about the author

Wladimir Kaminer was born in Moscow in 1967. After training as a sound engineer, studying drama and finishing his military service, he secured a visa and started a new life in Berlin in 1990. Written in his new-found language, *Russian Disco* became a huge bestseller in Germany. It was followed by the equally successful *Military Music*, a humorous memoir of his wayward youth in Moscow. His work has now been translated into eleven different languages. Kaminer is equally famous as a DJ at the Russian Disco, a compulsory weekly event for young Berliners which prompted *Marie Claire* to name him one of the six most important people in Berlin. Wladimir Kaminer lives in Berlin with his wife and children.

RUSSIAN DISCO

WLADIMIR KAMINER

translated by
Michael Hulse

EBURY
PRESS

7 9 10 8

Copyright © 2002 Wladimir Kaminer
Translation by Michael Hulse © Ebury Press

First published 2002 by Ebury Press,
An imprint of Random House,
20 Vauxhall Bridge Road, London SW1V 2SA
www.randomhouse.co.uk

Random House Australia (Pty) Limited
20 Alfred Street, Milsons Point, Sydney,
New South Wales 2061, Australia

Random House New Zealand Limited
18 Poland Road, Glenfield, Auckland 10, New Zealand

Random House (Pty) Limited
Isle of Houghton, Corner of Boundary Road & Carse O'Gowrie,
Houghton 2198, South Africa

The Random House Group Limited Reg. No. 954009

Printed and bound in Great Britain by Cox and Wyman

A CIP catalogue record for this book is available from the British Library.

Cover designed by Jon Gray

ISBN 9780091886691 (from January 2007)
ISBN 0091886694

Contents

Russians in Berlin

In the summer of 1990, a rumour was doing the rounds in Moscow: Honecker was taking Jews from the Soviet Union, by way of a kind of compensation for East Germany's never having paid its share of the German payments to Israel. According to the official East German propaganda, all the old Nazis were living in West Germany. The many dealers who flew from Moscow to West Berlin and back every week on import-export business brought the news back to the city with them. Word got around quickly. Everyone knew, except maybe Honecker. Normally most people in the Soviet Union tried to cover up any Jewish forebears they had, because you only had hopes of a career if your passport didn't give you away. The roots of this lay not in anti-Semitism but simply in the fact that every position that carried any responsibility at all required membership of the Communist Party. And nobody really wanted Jews in the Party. The whole Soviet people marched in step, like the soldiers on Red Square— from one triumph of Soviet labour to the next. No one could opt out, unless he was a Jew. As such, in theory at least, one might emigrate to Israel. If a Jew wanted to do just that, it was almost in order. But if a member of the Party applied for permission to emigrate, the other Communists in his branch lost face.

My father, for instance, was a candidate for Party membership four times, and every time he failed to get in. For ten years he was deputy manager of the planning department in a small business, dreaming of one day making it to manager. In that event he would have earned a whole 35 roubles more. But for the director, a manager of the planning department who wasn't a Party member was the stuff of nightmares. It wouldn't have worked in any case because the manager had to report on his work to the district committee of the Party assembly once a month. How on earth was he even to get in without a membership card?

Every year my father made a fresh attempt to join the Party. He drank vodka by the litre together with Party activists, he sweated to death with them in the sauna, but it was all in vain. Every year his schemes foundered on the same rock: 'We really like you, Viktor. You're our bosom pal for all time,' said the activists. 'We'd have liked to have you in the Party. But you know yourself that you're a Jew and might bugger off to Israel any moment' 'But I'll never do any such thing,' answered my father. 'Of course you won't, we all know that, but in theory it's possible, isn't it? Just think how stupid we'd all look.' And so my father never got past being a candidate for membership.

The new era dawned. Now the free ticket to the big wide world, the invitation to make a fresh start, was yours if you were Jewish. Jews who had formerly paid to have the word 'Jew' removed from their passports now started shelling out to have it put in. Suddenly every business wanted a Jewish world. Many people of various nationalities suddenly wanted to be Jews and emigrate to America, Canada or Austria. East Germany joined the list a little later on, and was something of an insider tip.

I got the tip from the uncle of a friend who sold photocopiers he imported from West Berlin. On one occasion we visited him in his apartment, which was already completely empty because the entire family were shortly to be departing for Los Angeles. All that remained was a large, expensive TV set with integrated video recorder, which still sat squarely on the floor in the middle of the room. The uncle was reclining on a mattress, watching porn movies.

'Honecker is taking Jews in East Berlin. It's too late for me to change course, I've already moved my millions to America,' he told us. 'But you're still young, you don't have anything, Germany's just the job for you, it's crawling with layabouts. They've got a stable welfare system. They won't even notice a couple more lads.'

The decision was taken spontaneously. In any case, it was far easier to emigrate to Germany than to America: the train ticket cost only 96 roubles, and for East Berlin you didn't need a visa. My friend Mischa and I arrived at Lichtenberg station in the summer of 1990. In those days one was still given a most democratic reception. In view of our birth certificates, which bore in black and white the information that both of us had Jewish parents, we were issued special certifications by an office specially established for the purpose in Marienfelde, West Berlin. These stated that we were recognised by Germany as citizens of Jewish origin. With these papers we then proceeded to the East German police headquarters on Alexanderplatz, and there, being recognised Jews, we were given an East German identity card.

In Marienfelde and at the Berlin Mitte police headquarters we met like-minded Russians, the vanguard of the fifth wave of emigrants. The first wave was the White Guard during the Revolution and the Civil War; the second wave emigrated between 1941 and 1945; the third consisted of expatriated dissidents in the Sixties; and the fourth wave commenced with Jews who migrated via Vienna in the Seventies.

The Russian Jews of the fifth wave in the early Nineties were indistinguishable from the rest of the German population by their creed or by their appearance. They might be Christians or Muslims or even atheists; they might be blond, red-heads or dark-haired; their noses might be snub or hooked. Their sole distinguishing feature was that, according to their passports, they were Jews. It was sufficient if a single member of the family was Jewish, or a half or quarter Jewish, and could prove as much in Marienfelde.

As with any game of chance, a good deal of cheating went on. Among the first hundred were people from every walk of life: a surgeon from the Ukraine with his wife and three daughters, an undertaker from Vilnius, an old professor who had done the calculations for the metal casings of the Russian sputniks and told anyone and everyone all about it, an opera singer with a funny voice, a former policeman, and a whole bunch of younger folk, 'students' such as ourselves.

A large aliens home was established for us in three prefab blocks in Marzahn that had once served East Germany's security service, the Stasi, as some kind of leisure centre. There we could now enjoy our leisure till further notice. The first in line always get the best deal. Once Germany had definitively been reunified, the newly arrived Jews were evenly distributed around the federal states. From the Black Forest to the woods of Thuringia, from Rostock to Mannheim. Every state had its own rules governing their admission.

In our cosy home in Marzahn we heard the wildest stories. In Cologne, for instance, the rabbi at the synagogue was asked to assess just how Jewish these new Jews really were. Unless they got a signed testimonial from him, there was nothing doing. The rabbi asked one lady what Jews ate at Easter. 'Gherkins,' said the lady: 'gherkins and Easter cake.' 'What makes you think they eat gherkins?' demanded the rabbi, agitated. 'Oh, right, now I know what you mean,' returned the lady, beaming. 'At Easter we Jews eat matzos.' 'Well, fair enough, the fact of the matter is that Jews eat matzos all year round, and that means they eat them at Easter too. But tell me,' enquired the rabbi, 'do you actually know what matzos are?' 'Of course I do,' replied the lady, delighted, 'they're those biscuits baked to an ancient recipe, with the blood of little children.' The rabbi fainted clear away. There were men who circumcised themselves purely to avoid questions like these.

We, being the first arrivals in Berlin, didn't have to undergo any of this. Only one prick in our home came to grief, and that was Mischa's. Berlin's Jewish community discovered our settlement in Marzahn and invited us to dinner every Saturday. Their attentions were lavished on the younger emigrants in particular. Cut off from the outside world, and lacking a knowledge of the language, we led a fairly isolated life in those days. The local Jews were the only people who took any interest in us. Mischa, my new friend Ilya and I went every week. A large table was always set, with a couple of bottles of vodka waiting for us. There was not much to eat, but everything had been prepared for the occasion with loving care.

The principal of the community liked us. Every now and then he'd want to give us 100 marks, and insisted we visit him at home. I didn't accept the money, because I realised that what was involved was not friendship pure and simple, though I found him and the other members of the community likeable. But they were a religious community in quest of new members. Once you enter into a relationship of that kind, sooner or later you are expected to give something in return. So on Saturdays I stayed in the home, roasting chestnuts in the gas oven and playing cards with the pensioners. My two friends, however, kept on going to the community gatherings and delighting in the presents they were given. They became friends with the principal and lunched at his home on several occasions. One day he said to them: 'You have shown yourselves to be good Jews, so now you have only to be circumcised and everything will be perfect.' 'Forget it,' Ilya shot back, and was gone. Mischa, who was of a more thoughtful disposition, stayed. He was tormented by his conscience on account of the cash he had accepted and the friendship of the principal, so now it was he who atoned for all our sins in the Jewish hospital in Berlin. Later he told us it hadn't hurt at all and even claimed it had heightened his sexual prowess.

For two weeks he was going about with a little tube peeping out of a surgical dressing. At the end of the third week, half the male residents in the home assembled in the washroom, hardly able to contain their curiosity. Mischa presented his prick to our view—as smooth as a sausage. With pride he expounded the nature of the operation: the foreskin was removed by laser, absolutely painless. But his prick left most of those present disappointed. They had expected something more, and their advice to Mischa was to let this Jewish business alone, advice he subsequently took. Some of the residents in the home were uneasy about the future and returned to Russia.

At that time, no one could understand why the Germans were choosing to accept us, of all people. In the case of the Vietnamese, say, whose home was also in Marzahn, not far from our own, it was perfectly understandable: they were the migrant workers of the East. But Russians? Perhaps police headquarters on Alexanderplatz had misunderstood something when they processed the first Jews, got it wrong, and ever since the worthy officers had been carrying on regardless, rather than admit their mistake? Much as they did when the Wall came down? But, like all dreams, this one was soon over. Just six months later, no more admissions were being made on the spot. Applications now had to be made in Moscow, and then you'd have a year or so to wait. Then quotas were introduced. At the same time, all Jews who had immigrated up to 31 December 1991 were granted refugee status and all the rights of citizenship except the right to vote.

These Jews and the Russian Germans constituted the fifth wave, though the Russian Germans are another story entirely. All the other groups taken together—Russian wives or husbands, Russian scientists, Russian prostitutes, students on scholarships—don't add up to a single per cent of my countrymen living here.

How many Russians are there in Germany? The editor-in-chief of Berlin's biggest Russian newspaper puts it at three million. And 140,000 in Berlin alone. But he is never quite sober, so I give no credence to what he says. After all, three years ago he was already putting the figure at three million. Or was it four? But it's true that the Russians are everywhere. The old editor is right, there are a lot of us, especially in Berlin. Every day I see Russians in the street, in the underground, in the bars, everywhere. One of the women who works on the tills at the supermarket where I do my shopping is Russian.

There's another at the hairdresser's. The salesgirl at the florist's is Russian too. Grossman the lawyer, though you would hardly believe it, originally came from the Soviet Union, just as I did ten years ago.

Yesterday in a tram two youths were having a loud conversation in Russian, thinking that no one could understand what they were saying. 'I'll never do it with a 200mm. There are always lots of people around him.' 'Then use a 500.' 'But I've never worked with a 500.' 'Fine, I'll call the boss tomorrow and ask for the instruction manual for a 500. But I don't know how he'll react. You'd be better trying with the 200. You can always try again.' Right.

Presents from East Germany

For a long time, my parents and I lived behind the Iron Curtain. Our only link to the West was the TV programme 'International Panorama', which went out on Channel One every Sunday right after 'Agricultural Round-Up'. The presenter, an overweight and always mildly stressed political analyst, had been on the road for years on important business: explaining the rest of the world to my parents and millions of other grown-ups. Every week he set out to spotlight on screen the whole range of contradictions inherent in capitalism. But the man was so fat that you could hardly see the foreign parts behind him.

'Over there, behind the bridge, the hungry unemployed are sleeping in old cardboard boxes, while up on the bridge, as you can see, the rich are driving by on their way to their places of recreation!' Fatty would report in a programme on New York—City of Contrasts. We stared at the screen as if we'd been hypnotised: up at the top you could see a bit of the bridge and one or two cars crossing it. These mysterious foreign parts didn't look particularly appealing, our man couldn't be having an easy time of it over there. But for some reason the political analyst didn't want to pack in his job, despite all the misery and squalor of the Western world, and kept on going back year in, year out. If the countries he happened to be visiting were poor, he praised the values of collectivisation and solidarity. Reporting from Africa, for instance, Fatty would say: 'Over there, behind my back, monkeys are attacking people, and monkeys are invincible because they stick together.'

Our family had another semi-legal source of information about life in foreign parts: Uncle Andrei on the third floor. He was a big cheese in the union of some secret works and it was no problem for him to travel to union meetings in Poland or even East Germany. Which he did at least twice a year. Every now and then Uncle Andrei and his wife came round to see my parents, invariably with a bottle of foreign schnapps. They barricaded themselves in the kitchen and our neighbour told them what it was really like abroad. Needless to say, the children were not allowed to listen. I was quite good friends with Uncle Andrei's son Igor; we were in the same class. Igor wore all kinds of foreign things: El Pico jeans, brown running shoes, even sleeveless T-shirts, which you could not get at home. Though Igor was the best-dressed boy in our class, he didn't boast about it, nor was he mean. Whenever I went to see him he'd give me some little thing or other. Before long I had a whole collection of what I called 'presents from East Germany', consisting of beer mats (the point and purpose of which was utterly beyond me), a bag of gummy bears, an empty Orient brand cigarette pack, an audio cassette, a stick of Lolek and Bolek chewing gum, and a transfer featuring some cartoon characters I was unfamiliar with. Igor wanted to be a union official one day like his father.

Once my father helped Uncle Andrei repair his Volga. In exchange he received a bottle of blue Curaçao, partly empty. The blue fluid had a powerful effect on my father's view of the world in those days. Not that he drank it. But by the blue light of the bottle, which stood on our bookshelf for quite some time, he grew more and more suspicious of the political analyst who presented 'International Panorama'. The presenter himself began to change as well. He became more thoughtful, and was increasingly at a loss for words to describe foreign places. In 1986, under Gorbachev, he suddenly disappeared from the TV screen. Doubtless he stayed for good in some land of contrasts or other. Not long after, the Iron Curtain came down, everything changed, the blue Curaçao gradually turned grey, and the world began to show its true face.

Father's Advice

In Russia we treasure every new idea and every scrap of ancient wisdom as our national heritage, something to be handed down from generation to generation.

The notion that I should move was my father's. It was 1990 and the Gorbachev era was gradually drawing to a close, though he didn't realise it. My father did, though. One sunny day over a beer he announced: 'Great Liberty has returned to our country. People are celebrating her arrival, the singing never stops, and neither does the drinking—with a vengeance. But Liberty is only passing through. She never does stay in Russia for long. Son, grab your chance. Don't just sit around drinking beer. The greatest of all freedoms is the opportunity to get out of here. Best get a move on. Once Liberty has made herself scarce again, you'll have all the time in the world to stand around wailing: "O blessed moment, stay, you are so fair!"'

My friend Mischa and I went to Berlin. Mischa's girlfriend flew to Rotterdam, his brother moved to Miami, and Gorbachev went to San Francisco. He knew someone in America. For us, Berlin was the simplest. You didn't need a visa to go there, not even a passport, because at that date it wasn't yet a part of the Federal Republic. The train journey cost only 96 roubles. It wasn't far to where we were headed. To raise the money for the ticket I sold my Walkman and my cassettes of Screamin' Jay Hawkins. Mischa sold his record collection.

I didn't have much in the way of luggage: a smart blue suit that a pianist had handed down to me, 200 Russian cigarettes, and some photos of my days in the army. With what was left of my money I bought a few souvenirs at the market in Moscow: a Russian doll lying pale-faced in a tiny coffin—I thought it was funny—and a bottle of Farewell brand vodka.

Mischa and I met at the station. He didn't have much with him either. At that time a lot of Russians were on the move, trying to sell this and that, and half the train consisted of romantics like ourselves, looking for adventure. The two days of the journey just flew by. The vodka with 'farewell' on the label was drained, the cigarettes were smoked, and the Russian doll vanished in mysterious circumstances. When we alighted at Lichtenberg station, it took us a few hours to get our bearings in our new surroundings. I was hungover and my blue suit was crumpled and stained. Mischa's leather waistcoat, which he had won off a Pole playing cards in the train, was also in urgent need of a clean. Our plan was simple: meet some people, establish contacts, find somewhere to live in Berlin. The first Berliners we got to know were gypsies and Vietnamese. We quickly struck up friendships.

The Vietnamese took Mischa along to Marzahn, where they were living in a home for aliens. There in the midst of the Marzahn jungle they raised him, just as Tarzan once grew up in the movie. The first words he learned here were Vietnamese. Now he is doing media studies at the Humboldt

University of Berlin, and takes offence whenever I call him Tarzan.

Back then, I went along with the gypsies and ended up in Biesdorf, where they were living in what had been an East German army barracks and had now been converted into a home by the German Red Cross. At the entrance I had to surrender my Russian ID. In exchange I got a bed to sleep in, and a foil-wrapped meal with the legend 'guten appetit'.

The gypsies felt just fine behind the barbed wire of the barracks. Right after lunch they would all head off into the city to do their business. In the evenings they would return with a sack full of cash and, often enough, an old car too. They never counted the money in the sack, they simply spent it at a pub in Biesdorf. It paid for drinks for the whole night. Then the tougher among them would get in the old car and crash it into a tree on the big yard behind the barracks. That was the climax of the night's fun. After a fortnight I was fed up with the gypsy life. I decided I wanted a steady bourgeois existence and moved to Prenzlauer Berg, where I found a tiny empty flat in Lychener Strasse, with an outside toilet. There I led a squatter's life till later I got married and rented a big apartment in Schönhauser Allee, and my wife had two children, and I learned an honest profession and began to write.

A First Apartment of My Own

For an eternity I had been dreaming of an apartment of my own. But it wasn't till the fall of the Wall that my dream came true. In the summer of 1990, once my friend Mischa and I had been recognised as members of a Jewish minority who had fled the Soviet Union, we ended up by a circuitous route in the enormous aliens' home that had been established in Marzahn. Hundreds of Vietnamese, Africans and Russian Jews were quartered there. The two of us and a friend from Murmansk, Andrei, managed to secure a one-room furnished apartment on the ground floor.

The home was all life and bustle. The Vietnamese discussed their future prospects in Vietnamese, not yet knowing anything about flogging cigarettes. The Africans cooked couscous all day long and in the evening sang Russian folk songs. Their knowledge of the language was amazingly good. A lot of them had studied in Moscow. The Russian Jews discovered six-packs of beer at 4.99 marks, traded cars among themselves, and made their preparations for a long winter in Marzahn. A lot of the residents complained to the staff that the people sharing their apartments weren't really Jews; they ate pork and went jogging round the block on Saturdays, which a genuine Jew would never do. These complaints were an attempt to get rid of their neighbours and have the assigned Stasi accommodation all to themselves. It was a regular war for space. Late-comers had a particularly hard time of it: they had to share their apartments with as many as four other families.

The three of us weren't especially charmed by life in the home and cast about for an alternative. In those days the Prenzlauer Berg part of Berlin was considered an insider tip for people looking for a place to live. The magic of those times when the Wall first came down hadn't yet come to an end there. The locals were heading for the West in droves and their flats were available, though they were crammed full of everything imaginable. At the same time a veritable counter-wave was arriving in the area from the West: punks, foreigners, members of the Church of the Holy Mother, weirdos, every kind of adept at the art of getting by. They moved into the flats, tossed the model railways that had been left behind on the garbage dump, stripped off the wallpaper and broke through the walls.

The housing authority had no idea what was going on any more. The three of us roamed from one building to the next, staring in at the windows. Andrei became the lucky owner of a two-room apartment in Stargarder Strasse, with an inside toilet and shower. Mischa found an empty flat in Greifenhagener Strasse, admittedly with neither a lavatory nor a shower but with a music centre and huge speakers, which suited his interests far better. I moved to Lychener Strasse. Herr Palast, whose nameplate was still on the door, had been in a distinct hurry. He had left almost everything behind: clean bed linen, a thermometer by the window, a clean fridge, and even a tube of toothpaste on the kitchen table. A little late in the day, I'd like to take this opportunity of thanking Herr Palast for everything. I'm especially grateful to him for the continuous-flow water heater he constructed himself, truly a technological miracle.

Two months later the days of squatting on the Prenzlauer Berg were over. The housing authority awoke from its torpor and declared everyone living in the buildings at that moment to be the rightful tenants. They would be provided with proper tenancy agreements. For the first time, I stood in line with two hundred others, all of them punks, freaks, holier-than-thou locals and feral foreigners. According to the rent agreement I would be paying 18.50 marks a month for my apartment. And that was how my dream came true: a room of my own, all 25 square metres of it.

My Father

When my mother and I left Moscow in 1990, my father was overjoyed. He'd killed two birds with one stone. For one thing, he was proud to have found his family a berth in the safety of exile in these difficult times. It had involved a certain amount of self-sacrifice and, all in all, had not been easy. Not everyone managed it. For another thing, after thirty years of marriage he finally had some peace and quiet and could do as he pleased. He was an engineer, and when the company he worked for went belly-up, as almost every small business did in the post-Soviet period of early capitalism, my father quickly hit on a solution. He drove around the city and discovered two tobacconists that charged very different prices for identical items. So in the mornings he'd buy at the one store, and in the afternoons he'd sell at the other. For a while he got by nicely in this way.

He reacted like a child to every novelty the market economy brought with it, without ever being especially surprised or regretful. When the crime rate soared to ever greater heights, he boarded up all the windows. He transformed the corridor into an arsenal: crowbars, knives, an axe, and a bucket for enemy blood, were all at the ready. In the bathtub my father hoarded food stores. He converted the kitchen into a lookout. Most of our items of furniture he chopped up into small pieces, one after another, in case there should be a sudden energy crisis. Whatever the news on TV, the confusions of the Perestroika era left my father cold. In the long run, though, his fortress became his prison. In 1993, worn out, he decided that he too would move to Berlin, in order to reunite the family: 'Familienzusammenführung' was the long German word noted in his passport.

Once here, he fell prey to depression, because after his long and arduous struggle he had nothing to do any more, surely the worst thing that can happen to you at sixty-eight. Simply to enjoy the sweet fruits of advanced capitalism went against the grain. My father longed for new tasks, for responsibility, for a life-or-death struggle.

Seek and ye shall find. And so my father hit on the idea of taking his driving test. It gave him something to keep him busy for the next couple of years. Three times he changed driving school. His first instructor leapt out of the car in the midst of moving traffic, swearing in three languages. The second submitted a written refusal to occupy the same vehicle as my father. 'Herr Kaminer looks at his feet all the time whilst driving,' he complained in his letter to the head of the driving school. Of course that was a lie. It was true enough that my father's eyes were never on the street when he was driving but were fixed somewhere down below. But he wasn't staring at his feet, he was keeping an eye on the pedals so he didn't step on the wrong one.

The third instructor was a man of mettle. Once he and my father had spent several hours together in the car and had looked Death in the eye, they were like brothers. This instructor finally managed to talk my father out of the notion of getting his driving licence.

Another long period of depression ensued, till he discovered 'Die Knallschoten', a cabaret act in the Weissensee part of Berlin, by and for senior citizens. He promptly joined. In their new programme entitled 'No reason to keep quiet'—a satire on problems of the present day, 'fun but with a sting in the tail!'—my father plays the foreigner. I never miss a show and always take him a fresh bunch of flowers.

My Mother on her Travels

My mother spent the first sixty years of her life in the Soviet Union. Not once did she cross the borders of her homeland, despite the fact that in 1982 her best friend, who married a German stationed in Moscow and moved with him to Karl Marx Stadt, repeatedly invited my mother to visit her there. The Party Secretary at the Institute of Mechanical Engineering where she worked would have had to sign the assessment that was needed if she were to make such a journey, and he never did so. 'Foreign travel is an honour and carries responsibility,' he told my mother every time. 'You, however, have not been conspicuous in the field of social or political work, Mrs Kaminer. I conclude that you are not yet ready to undertake a journey of this sort.'

Only when the Soviet Union collapsed was my mother 'ready to undertake a journey of this sort'. She emigrated to Germany in 1991. She quickly discovered one of the great liberties afforded by democracy: freedom of movement. Now she could go anywhere. But how far does one really want to go, and how big is the world to be? The answers to these questions were supplied pretty much of their own accord once my mother familiarised herself with the tour programme of Roland Reisen, a cheap bus tours operator in Berlin. No buses go to America, Australia or India, that's for sure. But there are still long journeys to be made. You have the feeling you are embarking on far-flung travels yet at the same time you're somehow still close to home. It's practical, economical and fun. Roland Reisen tours, though popular, are often cancelled due to lack of bookings, but even so my mother has now been on around two dozen bus tours to quite a number of destinations, from Spain in the south to Denmark in the north.

In Copenhagen she photographed the Little Mermaid, who happened to be lacking her head once again. In Vienna the tour guide told my mother that Wiener sausages were called Frankfurters there, and moreover that the only decent coffee to be had was in the restaurant by the town hall, and that Stapo was an abbreviation for the police. In Paris the bus driver couldn't find anywhere to park so they sat in the bus all day, driving round and round the Eiffel Tower. At Lake Wolfgang my mother bought genuine Mozart Kugeln, the roundest pralines in the world, which she has been giving me for Christmas ever since. On Charles Bridge in Prague they came close to colliding with another tour bus. In Amsterdam it happened to be the Queen's birthday and lots of blacks were dancing for joy in the streets when my mother arrived in the Roland Reisen bus. In Verona she viewed the memorial to Shakespeare's Juliet, whose left breast has been left small and shiny by the hands of countless tourists. My mother wasn't able to take a trip to London, though, because Britain is not part of the Schengen Agreement and it wasn't till she was in Calais that she realised that she required a special visa for the UK. She ended up spending twenty-four hours photographing every other building in Calais, and next day when the bus passed through on the return leg my mother climbed aboard for the ride back to Berlin.

The fact that she had not even got close to Big Ben and Tower Bridge didn't trouble her greatly. She now knows the ropes of bus travel, and for her to travel is a more important thing than to arrive.

The Sweet Homeland Far Away

My wife Olga was born on the island of Sakhalin, in the town of Okha—1,000 kilometres from Tokyo, 10,000 kilometres from Moscow, 12,000 from Berlin. In the town there were three primary schools numbered 5, 4 and 2. Number 3 was missing, and rumour in Okha had it that the school was swept into the sea by a snowstorm thirty years ago, because it had one floor too many. Close to the three schools were the town's penal and reform institutions: near school 5 was the law court, near school 4 the mental asylum, and near school 2 the prison. This proximity had a great educational impact and made it easy work for the strict teachers of Okha to tame the local youngsters. They had only to point or glance out of the window to remind their pupils of what lay in store for them if they didn't do their homework on time.

To the delight of the children there was no school whenever a snowstorm beset the island or the temperature dropped under minus 35 Celsius. Then they would all sit at home looking forward to the autumn vacation. For there were only two seasons on Sakhalin: the long winter and then, from the end of July, when the last of the snow thawed, the autumn. With the autumn came large numbers of ships bringing delicious treats such as dried watermelon rind for the kindergartens, so the children would have something to get their teeth into. From China there were dried pineapples, dried bananas, frozen plums and Chinese sandstorms. From Japan there were Japanese Big John jeans, which were invariably too small. Nevertheless, the people of Sakhalin always queued for them. Everyone went on about the Japanese, staggered that they could even survive with such short legs and such fat behinds. But every family had a sewing machine at home and altered the Big Johns to suit their own requirements.

The programme of entertainment on the island was fairly monotonous. In winter my wife sat with the other children in the only cinema on Sakhalin, the Oil Workers' Cinema, watching old Russian and German movies such as *Three Men in the Snow, Lost in the Ice* or *Three Friends on the High Seas*. The children were the first generation native to the island, apart from the Nivkhis, the aboriginals of Sakhalin, who were gradually nearing extinction on a reservation at the south of the island. The children's parents were all geologists or oil drillers, and came from all fifteen republics of the Soviet Union. In the autumn the children liked to go swimming. There were two lakes in the town, Pioneer Lake and Komsomol Members' Lake. Pioneer Lake was small, shallow and dirty, but Komsomol Members' Lake was a respectable depth and was clean. There was another place to go swimming too, known as Bear Lake, about two kilometres beyond the city limits, near Cape Calamity. But nobody dared go because of the racoons which had mutated through the influence of the Chinese sand-storms into dangerous amphibians, a kind of Sakhalin crocodile. Apart from the racoons there were other animals there too: brown bears, foxes, and any number of hares that lived in the big field behind the hospital. There were no wolves any more. The last Sakhalin wolf was shot at Cape Calamity in 1905. It was honoured with a concrete memorial, but at some point in a snowstorm this tipped over and fell into the water. Cape Calamity was so named not because of the wolf but because it marked the end of the trail, time and again, for prisoners who had escaped and were trying to make it to the mainland. Either they disappeared under the ice or they were shot by the soldiers.

All the adults on Sakhalin were paid the northern latitudes bonus, which doubled their pay. They were also entitled to retire earlier. Children on Sakhalin weren't even paid the regular rate. At the age of twelve, on the airfield at Khabarovsk, Olga saw a sparrow for the first time in her life. 'Mamma, Mamma, look at those huge flies,' she exclaimed. 'Those are sparrows, you daft Kartoga kid—not flies, sparrows,' a man snapped back in some agitation. To judge by his appearance he had just served a sentence and was waiting for the next plane south. He laughed, drew greedily on his cigarette and swore. 'Bloody sparrows, bloody country, bloody kids, bloody taiga!'

When she was sixteen, Olga finished school and flew to Leningrad to learn a sensible trade. A few years later she moved to Germany, which is a terribly long way from her homeland, it's true, but even so she has a lot of time for Berlin.

My Wife Alone at Home

My Olga is a plucky person. She lived for a long time in the Chechen capital, Grozny, so now she is afraid of next to nothing. Her parents were geologists and spent fifteen years on Sakhalin looking for oil and mineral deposits. Olga went to school there. In eighth grade, since she was top of the class, she got a reward. She was flown on an outing to the tiny island of Iturup, by helicopter. Shortly after she arrived, the infamous eruption of the volcano, Mount Iturup, occurred. Olga played her part: that is to say, she ran around the island screaming, with the fishing folk who lived there. In the taiga of Sakhalin, Olga was chased by bears and other wild animals on several occasions. Even as an infant she could handle a gun.

When their contracted term on Sakhalin was over, her parents bought a little house on the outskirts of their home city, Grozny. It was just before the war broke out. When the Chechen uprising began in the city, the house was surrounded by Chechen rebels and fired on. Her parents defended their property and shot back with their hunting rifles, from every window of the house, out into the dark Caucasian night. Olga's job was reloading. She had to fight for her life on other occasions later, too. Now she has been living for ten years in the peaceful city of Berlin; but her appetite for great deeds has not quite deserted her.

I happened not to be at home when there was a sudden power cut. It wasn't only our building that was affected: the whole of Prenzlauer Berg had no electricity. There had been a short circuit, and for an hour the entire district was without power. It was almost like a real natural disaster; bank cards refused to emerge from cash dispensers, cinema shows stopped dead, traffic lights were out of action, and even the trams weren't running. But my wife had no knowledge of any of this. When the flat was plunged into darkness, she simply decided to solve the problem herself. Candle in hand, she descended to the cellar, where the fuse-box was. Outstretched on the floor below the fuse-box lay a man, motionless. 'That must be the electrician,' my wife promptly decided; 'he must have disregarded the safety regulations and the short will have killed or at least seriously hurt him.'

Quickly she ran back up the steps and knocked on all the doors, requesting the neighbours in loud tones to help her carry the electrician upstairs. But the neighbours were all secure in their darkened apartments and had no intention of helping to retrieve the dead electrician. The only ones who opened their door were the Vietnamese on the first floor. But they too were afraid to go down into the dark cellar with my wife. And so she decided to drag the electrician out of the cellar all by herself. She had a suspicion that his body might still be live with voltage, so she borrowed a pair of rubber gloves from the Vietnamese. Then down she went again, heaved the man up, and hefted him up the steps. In her arms, the dead electrician began to show signs of life. When the two of them had reached the second floor, the power came back on. Under the electric light, the half-dead electrician proved to be a boozed-up wino who had found himself a cosy spot in our cellar. Once he had come round, he politely asked my wife if she could spare him any change, given that she was already carrying him around. My wife stood there on the staircase somewhat embarrassed, still wearing the rubber gloves, holding the candle in one hand and the wino in the other. Even the Vietnamese, who usually keep very much to themselves, had a good laugh at her. Nowadays it isn't so easy to satisfy an appetite for great deeds.

My First Frenchman

The first Frenchman I got to know in Berlin was called Fabrice Godar. The two of us and an Arab girl were hired for a theatre project, on a government-subsidised job scheme. He was a cameraman, I was a sound technician, and the girl was a seamstress. The government subsidies were aimed at giving work to the lower strata of the people, who would otherwise hardly have a chance in the job market: the elderly, the handicapped, and foreigners.

The North Berlin job centre had written to tell me to go to a pub, the Krähe, for a job interview at 10 p.m. So I went. About a dozen men and women were sitting at a long table. A fellow with a moustache, a cigar and a glass of whisky in his hand was the ringleader. This wasn't Heiner Müller or Jochen Berg, however, nor was it Thomas Brasch or Frank Castorf. This man had a strong resemblance to Che Guevara and was planning a theatre revolution.

With my Russian accent I got the job on the spot. Fabrice got a job too and we were soon mates. He measured up perfectly to the clichéd picture I had of a Frenchman: he was thoughtless, superficial, open-minded, and fixated on women. We sang the Internationale together and Fabrice told me he was still a virgin.

Some time or other he decided he would take advantage of this government-subsidised project to get rid of his virginity once and for all, and became Sabine's lover. She was married to one of the actors, a man ten years older than Fabrice, and they had a grown-up son. For her it was a little adventure; for Fabrice, however, it was his first great love, with all that that entails. Their relationship came to an end a little later in a truly French fashion. The husband came home from rehearsals earlier than expected. Sabine hid Fabrice in the wardrobe. An hour or so later the husband wanted to change, opened his wardrobe, and discovered the French cameraman within.

A Frenchman in the wardrobe: ridiculousness of such an order ought to be confined to comic movies. In this case, however, it was sad rather than silly. Sabine's husband went to the theatre and informed everyone that, following this incident, he would no longer be capable of playing the principal role in our Brecht play. And this was two weeks before the premiere! All of us went round to Sabine to thrash out the matter together. She was very understanding, and struck Fabrice off her list of lovers. After which, the Frenchman broke down totally. He no longer turned up at the theatre, and grew ever more depressed. One day he couldn't stand it any more and went to a psychotherapist, whom he told everything about Sabine and the wardrobe, saying that he could not sleep since it had happened. The doctor promptly asked him how long he had been unemployed. Quite a time, Fabrice replied, but that had nothing to do with it. The doctor was of an entirely different opinion and prescribed him a new antidepressant with a long-term effect, developed in Germany specifically for the treatment of people who take early retirement or the long-term unemployed, who have problems sleeping and suffer from depression. 'Come and see me again in six months' time and we'll see how things are getting on,' the doctor said in soothing tones.

The effect of the jab held. Fabrice became indifferent. He slept like a baby and spent the rest of his time watching DSF, the German sports channel, on television. He forgot to go shopping or to wash, and didn't even call his father in France any more, which he had previously done once a fortnight. We were all extremely concerned about him, but did not quite know how to help. One day his father turned up in a big Citroën and took Fabrice back to France. There the French doctors at some specialist clinic managed to counteract the effects of the German injection. Fabrice recovered his health and now works for the post office, like his father.

The Everyday Life of a Work of Art

It was autumn when I first met the Russian sculptor Sergei N. at an exhibition opening in the Berlin Academy of Fine Arts. A man of thirty-five, composed, self-confident and assured. We were both pleased, since it is always good to meet a fellow countryman abroad, and an artist to boot. His eyes alight, Sergei described what he was working on. It seemed that for years he had worked only with concrete. He held lighter materials in contempt, he told me. The work was called Mother Heart and represented a medium-sized seashell with a point in the middle from which several beams radiated out. I recognised immediately that Sergei was a man of great gifts. The Mother Heart posed an immense question to all mankind: Why? A heart of concrete, the suffering of matter and the passion of stone.

We had tea together and talked about art. I asked Sergei what his work meant. He shook his head and said: 'Better if we go and have a vodka!' Subsequently I forgot about the enigmatic shell. It was winter now, and the first snow was falling. Sergei called and told me that he had entered his shell in the big competition for a Holocaust memorial. It symbolised all the pain of humanity in concentrated form, he said, a scream cast in concrete. I could well imagine the shell as a Holocaust memorial. We got together again, as this news clearly called for discussion. We talked about art, drank tea, and then moved on to vodka.

Some weeks later I heard from Sergei that his work had been turned down on the pretext that it was too small for a principal Holocaust memorial. He had nonetheless not given up the hope of finding the right place for his shell some day. For a while after that I would think about contemporary art, especially over a cup of tea, but then I forgot the whole business again.

Spring arrived and the days grew warmer once more. Sergei had been invited to Prague. His shell was to be placed as a memorial to the wholesale rape of Czech women by Soviet soldiers when they invaded Czechoslovakia in 1968. Sergei asked whether I thought it would be better to ship the shell to Prague by truck or train. We arranged to meet for tea, and sat together for a while talking about art and even planning to make the trip to Prague together. In the event, though, it didn't work out. A fortnight later, Sergei learned that the deal was off: the entire project was under reconsideration, for budget reasons. Back home I leafed through art magazines for some time after, but then I stopped and returned to everyday matters.

At last it was summer. The trees were in leaf again and the grass was growing. Sergei asked if I could help him transport his shell to Hamburg, to an erotica fair, where it would be expressing the unrequited desire for vaginal contact. We had terrific fun in Hamburg. The men flocked around Sergei's masterpiece, scratching at the concrete. A middle-aged woman stopped in her tracks when she saw the sculpture, flushed, and looked around uncertainly. A few days later we loaded the shell on the trailer and drove it back to Berlin. We were both hungover and went our separate ways. For a while the memory of Hamburg stayed with me, but then I forgot all about it.

Autumn came round, the days grew cooler, there were fewer people about in the streets. One day, wandering the city aimlessly, I happened upon an adventure playground in Wedding. The children were swarming all over a giant snail that rose out of the sand. Despite its fresh paint, I instantly recognised the Mother Heart of old. Some things you never forget. It looked magnificent as a snail in that playground. The children seemed thrilled with it too. Sergei had good reason to be pleased with himself and the world. I went home with a spring in my step and a song in my throat.

Out of the Garden of Love

In the late Eighties I often met up with other youths in the foyer of the Cinema of Movie Classics in Moscow. We were drop-outs and we all had nicknames. So did the foyer; it was known as the Garden of Love. It was called that because in winter it was warm there and hardly anyone went to the cinema. We met practically every day and talked about the most important matters. The subject that interested us most in those days was not girls or drugs but emigrating. Our biggest heroes were those who had managed to get across the border. Those were people we could somehow identify with, because all of us felt there was somebody after us: the police were after the older lads, and Mum and Dad were after the younger ones.

For one friend we called Prince, though, the subject took on obsessive proportions. He collected every newspaper report about escapees and meticulously stuck them into a scrapbook. He knew them all—the wily East German family that had sewn a hot-air balloon out of raincoats and flown across the border, the Estonian couple who coated themselves in goose fat and swam the 100 kilometres to Finland. They were in the cold water for two days, but after that they were in sunny Finland for the rest of their lives. Prince also knew the story of Sachanevich the painter, who dived off a ship while on a Black Sea cruise and made it to Turkey. He knew about Petrov the sculptor who had sprayed himself with bronze paint and pretended to be a statue awaiting shipment to an exhibition in Paris. Petrov spent a whole week in a crate but he never made it to Paris. A customs official opened up the crate at a stop in Amsterdam, because the stench of shit was overpowering. From it emerged the bronze-painted Petrov, requesting political asylum as a persecuted artist. Vitali, the Prince, dreamt of pulling off a similar coup and was preparing thoroughly for it. But my other friend, Andrei, known as the Pessimist, pronounced all Prince's ideas useless and laughed at him. 'We're in slavery here for ever. No matter how cleverly you plan your escape, the Soviets will fetch you back.'

It was a surprise to us all that Andrei proved the first to make a break out of the Garden of Love and into the big wide world. When the Pope visited Poland, the soldiers on the Polish border with White Russia couldn't keep the faithful back. A special regulation was hastily introduced to cope with them: pilgrims were permitted to enter Poland in small groups, using a list of names but without needing a stamp. In those days, with his beard and long hair, the lean Pessimist looked every inch the religious fanatic. He had no difficulty joining one of the groups of pilgrims. Barely were they across the border when he separated from them and travelled on to Germany, without giving the Pope so much as a glance. He managed to get as far as France, and when he was hitch-hiking near Paris he met a Russian who offered to help him. The Pessimist settled in Paris and worked in a Russian bookshop there. For the past five years he has been living off his painting.

Meanwhile Prince was to be found almost daily on Arbat, the main tourist street, chatting up elderly foreign ladies in pursuit of his latest escape plan. Women from Sweden or Finland were his preference, if at all possible. He had got the notion that in those countries there was a shortage of capable men. Just as he finally began to abandon hope, he met a girl from Denmark, a journalist. She ended up smuggling him back with her to Copenhagen. A little later I was sent a copy of the newspaper *Dagens Nyheter*, with his toothless grin on the front page. 'This man lost all his teeth on the streets of Moscow,' ran the headline. Prince told me in a letter that the Danish parliament had convened an extraordinary session on his account, and he was accorded political asylum. Recently he founded his own company.

In the meantime, both of my friends have become European, which is to say that they have changed a great deal. We communicate only rarely these days, and then by email.

The Sergeant's Wedding

A friend of mine, a former sergeant in the Soviet army, has been living illegally in Germany for the past ten years. In 1989, that all-important year for this country, he abandoned his post, then still a young sergeant, climbed over the fence, and hid out in the gym of a Mecklenburg primary school near his barracks. There he made contact with some of the pupils, explained his unfortunate situation to them, and exchanged his boots and uniform for a pair of gym shoes and sportswear. Dressed in this manner he managed to get to Berlin. Without any socks.

The next ten years of his life were distinctly placid. He got a job with a party catering company and rented a small room in a flat shared by Russians. A non-drinker and non-smoker by conviction, and disciplined by his long service in the army, he never had any brushes with the police, nor they with him. What was more, he even rose through the ranks at the caterers', from dish-washer to shift superintendent. After ten years of hard work and thrifty living the sergeant had managed to save the considerable sum of 20,000 marks, under his pillow. That money, he hoped, would provide the solution to what seemed the only problem he still had to tackle: re-entering society by legalising his status. But how was it to be done? The time-honoured canniness of all illegal immigrants told him a bogus marriage was the thing.

Taking advice, he decided to place a small ad. At first he was reluctant to betray his true intentions, and opted for a perfectly normal, 'typically German' style of personal ad. The sergeant studied the columns for months, to familiarise himself with the 'German way' of phrasing an ad, and at length inserted his one-liner in several publications simultaneously: 'Cuddly bear seeks cuddly mouse.'

The result was astounding. The poor sergeant was in greater demand than 'Elderly gentleman would like to hear from young women', which has been a staple in the Berlin small ads columns for years. Most of the cuddly mice turned out to be women over forty, with an over-complicated bundle of relationships in their baggage, and a stack of frustrations to match. Shy as he was, the sergeant did not feel equal to their problems, and pulled out every time.

Before long he changed his tactics. In the next ad he used the word 'reward', which he felt signalled the true intentions of the groom. Someone in Eberswalde called him, offering him a Russian-German woman for 10,000 marks. The sergeant went over to Eberswalde, where an entire village of Russian-Germans from Kazakhstan, from babes in arms to grandmothers, turned out to witness this quest for a bride. The sergeant, wary and suspicious after his long years of illegal living, pulled out once again. 'Russian women are so romantic,' he told me that evening over a glass of vodka. 'Even if they're only marrying for the money, they want everything to be just right for the groom, and want to be sure they look their best when he goes to inspect the bride.'

A little later the sergeant made the acquaintance of a broker, a Persian from Azerbaijan who assured him he could procure any sham bride he might conceivably want, from girls on welfare to professional working women, if need be, for the sum of 15,000 marks, and five years down the track he would conscientiously dispose of her.

'Two-thirds of the money goes to the woman and I get one-third. Come round and we'll talk it over man to man,' the Persian proposed enticingly. 'My office is in the Forum Hotel. And rest assured—I'm married to a German myself, she's even a lawyer, we work together.'

I smelt a whopper of a rat when I heard this story, and the sergeant changed his mind too when he was already in the lobby of the Forum Hotel, with the money on him, and turned on his heel. By now, the others he shares the flat with are all convinced he will never get married. He is simply too shy, too choosy, and furthermore too broody, they say. Right now he is making another attempt, and goes to a disco in Sophienstrasse every evening. He doesn't dance, he just stands at the bar, scrutinising everyone else. What he hopes to achieve by doing this, he hasn't told me.

Relationships in the Berlin Hothouse

It is often said that Berlin is the singles capital of Germany. But people in the city only laugh when they hear this. No one but some shallow-witted journalist who puts more faith in statistics than the evidence of his own eyes can suppose anything of the sort. The statistics are lies and always were lies. Statistics are used to lying. Berlin is not a city of singles. It is a city of relationships. To be precise, the city is one great romantic hothouse, that instantly draws in every newcomer. Everyone lives with everyone else. In winter the hothouse is invisible, but in spring you see it again. If you make the effort to trace the relationships of one solo person far enough back, before long you'll realise that the person in question, at least indirectly, has had a thing with the entire city.

Take our friend Marina—though any friend, of either sex, would be just as good an example. But let's take Marina anyway, because every evening she sits in our kitchen telling us the details of her private life. This involves us indirectly in her stories too. Marina, then. Last year, when her husband left her for a ballerina whose ballerino, away performing in

Munich, had suddenly fallen for his best friend's daughter, who was twenty-three, single, pregnant, and in the deepest depression because her boyfriend had run off with a beautiful Egyptian woman who worked for TUI, the package holidays company, and happened also to be called Tui. But back to Marina: her husband was gone and that meant there was a threat hanging over her whole life and livelihood. For about ten years, Marina had been studying satellite geodesy at the Technical University. She had studied and studied and had got so proficient that she could calculate the gravity of the planets Mars or Venus precisely simply by glancing out the window of a bar. Gravity, it seems, is different everywhere. But she still hadn't written her diploma dissertation. And now Marina urgently needed a job. At lightning speed she wrote her dissertation on some funny pair of twin satellites in orbit together around the Earth, and sent out three dozen job applications.

Presently a construction company in need of an engineer got in touch with her. Marina went for an interview and didn't come home. Her fourteen-year-old daughter was desperately worried and phoned us at midnight. It wasn't till the following day that Marina arrived home—with a new job, and a new man. The interview had been conducted in a garage, she told us later. The young builder had recently caught his wife with another man, and in frustration had moved out into the garage for the time being, with all his stuff. It was serving him as the office of his construction business too. So he'd just been through a rough time, and was looking for someone to help him get back on his feet. It was love at first sight. The interview was short, Marina landed the job on the spot, and they went to dinner together. The young businessman confided his secret dream to Marina: a house on the shores of the Black

Sea, with a veranda and a view of his own yacht. 'How would you feel about sitting on that veranda with me?' the man asked Marina in earnest tones. He was firmly resolved and wasn't going to take 'maybe' for an answer. 'Yes, maybe,' said Marina, 'if my daughter would be welcome there as well.' 'Your children will always have a place on my veranda,' the besotted businessman assured her.

Next day he moved out of the garage and into Marina's flat. At first everything seemed perfect. Marina met his parents, and even his ex-wife, who tore out a handful of her hair at their first encounter. But in the course of time the veranda came to feel more and more cramped. Marina couldn't handle a round-the-clock relationship for longer than a fortnight. The man moved back into the garage. Every day she took him something to eat when she went to work. One day on her way she met a nice policeman. Some person unknown had stolen an umbrella from her car, and the policeman who handled the matter fell in love with Marina there and then, and asked her to dinner. He called her every fifteen minutes, but in the event he didn't turn up to their date. Probably the officer was shot in the line of duty, thought Marina. Meanwhile her daughter had acquired her first boyfriend at school. He was a resourceful lad: he simply gave the daughter a mobile phone, and then bombarded her with red-hot email messages. Marina was distinctly concerned. Time and again she warned her daughter to be careful. No one knows for sure what today's new technology might be doing to you.

Which Marina's latest man, an Indian computer engineer, was happy to confirm.

The Russian Bride

Over the past ten years, which I have spent in Berlin, I have got to know a good many Russo-German married couples, and I believe I can claim that if there is one universal means of delivering a man from all of his problems at a single blow, then it is a Russian bride. Does your life seem boring? Are you out of work? Are you suffering from an inferiority complex, or acne? Get yourself a Russian bride and soon you won't know yourself.

For one thing, loving a Russian woman is a very romantic business, because there are any number of obstacles to be overcome before she is yours. For instance, you have to submit a declaration of income to the Aliens Office, to demonstrate that you can indeed afford a Russian bride. If not, the lady won't be issued a residence permit. An acquaintance of mine, who as a BVG employee apparently didn't make enough to be able to marry his Russian beloved, wrote dozens of letters to Chancellor Schröder and bombarded the Foreign Office with complaints. It was a tough struggle. But it was worth it: now the man has his bride and has been given a raise into the bargain.

What's more, I know a large number of Germans who had been unemployed and depressed for a long time and then speedily found a job and even embarked on successful careers simply because they had fallen in love with Russian women. But then, they had no option, because Russian brides are very, very demanding, not to say expensive. Not only do they invariably want to look good themselves but they also insist that the man always be dressed in the very latest style, which means he is forever having to buy new, expensive clothes. 'Is this really necessary?' the men ask, in the early days, but before long they submit readily enough. Simply everything has to be just so. For the wedding a Russian bride wants a white dress, a church, a register office, and afterwards a good restaurant with as many guests as possible. Thereafter she will devote herself entirely to family life, though she will also pursue some pretty studies or other at the same time. Such as singing, at a private academy. This is very popular with Russian brides. In Berlin alone I know three women who go to singing school, and it's not cheap!

The Russian bride inspires a man with courage, gives new meaning to his life, protects him from enemies if he has them, and always stands by him, even when he screws up. But in your everyday life with her, caution is advised. The Russian bride is sensitive and requires particular care and attention.

Unfortunately, conflict with her cannot simply be laid to rest with a bunch of flowers. It takes more. If the dispute is serious, the best thing is to run, quickly. When her fury is aroused, the Russian bride is a tigress. So it is most important to know exactly what the legal basis of a Russian bride's status is in the Federal Republic of Germany. The Russian department at Radio MultiKulti frequently covers this topic, in its programme 'A Lawyer Advises'.

'I recently married a young German and moved in with him,' a Russian woman will write from Celle, say, 'and now I have been given a residence permit for three years by the German authorities. If something were to happen to my husband suddenly, such as a fatal car crash, would my right of residence be rescinded or not?' 'In that eventuality, dear lady,' the lawyer advises, 'your right of residence would not be rescinded. But it would nonetheless be better if your husband were to remain alive another year or so.'

Love Rules the World

I was asked to assist the manager of the Palace of Tears night-club in a Russian affair of the heart. He had fallen in love with one of my countrywomen, in a brothel, and meant to get her out. She, however, neither spoke nor understood any German. When we met up, the woman, Diana, told me that in fact she was in love with another German entirely. I really should meet him, she assured me: Frank was a ventilation technician, and he too had discovered Diana in the brothel. The girl was from a White Russian village by the name of Goziki and had come to Berlin on a forged Polish passport to seek her fortune. Both of them had been absolutely bowled over when they met. It was love at first sight. Frank did not waste time think-ing it over and proposed to Diana. He knew he was taking a real risk, since he hardly knew the girl. But where he lived in Spandau he had the experience of a neighbour constantly before him, a construction engineer who had married a Czech prostitute and was getting along famously.

At all events, Diana at first turned down Frank's proposal. She was still very young and wanted to earn some decent money before later maybe settling down to start a family. The knocking shop where she earned her daily crust was not doing especially good business, though. The proprietor of the brothel was hopelessly in love with one of his girls. She was forever getting pregnant, but she didn't much care for the man. The proprietor was gradually losing the will to live. He got drunk every day, and was losing weight. The other girls tried to comfort him—and got pregnant as well. The brothel was turning into a fine hothouse of relationships.

One day the proprietor vanished, leaving the women to fend for themselves. The brothel was closed down. In desperation, Diana called the only regular customers she had: first the manager of the Palace of Tears, then the ventilation technician. In the end she turned up at his place in Spandau. This time she accepted his proposal. The technician took a week's sick leave and a 5,000-mark loan with the Noris Bank. Then off they both went to Goziki in White Russia, to get married. There Frank was promptly confronted with the savage customs of White Russia. Even before they had left the railway station, their luggage was stolen. The bridesmaids accused Diana of betraying her homeland and gave her a black eye. Frank was also attacked by some of the locals, on patriotic grounds. After this, though, everyone became the best of friends. The wedding was celebrated in the village's biggest hall, the primary school gym. Frank bought five crates of vodka for the men and five of port for the women. The merrymaking lasted two days and would have continued but for Diana's father ruining everything. Overjoyed, he went down to the River Goziki to go swimming, drunk as a newt— and never came back. People were kept busy a whole day trying to recover his body from the river. Slowly but surely the wedding festivities turned into a funeral wake.

Once this was over, the newly-weds returned to Berlin.

Diana was detained at the Polish-German border. It turned out that she was banned from entering the Schengen states because of the forged Polish passport she had previously been using. Frank was obliged to continue his journey alone. Every day he phoned the Aliens Office. He wrote to the Foreign Office, the Federal Chancellor, the Minister of Family Affairs, and the Supreme Court. And two months on, he achieved the impossible: the bureaucratic machinery, normally invincible, capitulated to their love, the ban on Diana's entering the country was lifted, and now she is in Berlin once more. And the moral of this story? Goethe was right after all: love really is stronger than anything else.

The Girl and the Witches

Even these days there are many people with a materialist view of life who still have a penchant for the metaphysical. They see a distinct significance in things that others consider unpleasant or beneath contempt. If someone is dissatisfied with himself, he promptly thinks his bed ought to be in a different corner of the room, or foreigners are to blame, or even extraterrestrials. Not to feel responsible oneself, and yet to find everything of interest, is a condition that we owe to metaphysics. We seek a miracle that will resolve all conflict, an immediate, once-and-for-all salvation.

When our Russian friend Marina's husband suddenly left her because he had fallen head over heels for a ballerina, after ten years of marriage, she was in a state of shock. It was the end of the world, she visibly lost weight and couldn't sleep properly any more. We saw a pretty funny side to the story, because Marina had been up in arms at the uncultured habits of her husband for an eternity. He was forever watching TV at home, showing not the remotest interest in intellectual public life. And what happened? One day the lout gave in and went to the ballet, and promptly fell for the first dancer he'd set eyes on in his life. The response of a forty-five-year-old man who had never previously seen a ballerina at close quarters might easily have been predicted. Be that as it may, Marina decided a spell had been cast on her by the late mother of her first husband, to be exact, and that she was doomed to die if we didn't manage to find her a witch in Berlin who could restore her to her healthy unhexed state.

Since I didn't know a thing about witching, I consulted a friend who was thought by our family to know what was what. Instantly he suggested two witches who he felt would be equal to the task, one a Chinese and one an African.

Madam U Ti received her clients at a shared medical practice. The brand of sorcery she practised was known as kinesiology. She claimed that for 30 marks she would discover what was wrong with Marina in next to no time. She took Marina's hands in her own and put questions to her muscles, in German with a light Chinese accent. The Russian muscles made a gentle, weakly response, but Madam U Ti understood them very clearly nevertheless. Once she had examined all Marina's limbs thoroughly, she announced that for a mere 60 marks she could prepare a medicinal extract for her ailing body. Marina lay down, and Madam U Ti placed a variety of glass phials on her breast, asking the body every time if this medicine was the right one. When the correct one had been found, Marina immediately began to feel better. She even joined in our laughter, and for a few days was perfectly cheerful. Even so, the sorcery disappointed her. She had expected something else entirely.

So we decided to give the African witch a try as well. She received us not in some catacombs with skulls piled high on the floor but in a three-room Berlin apartment with parquet floors and a well-upholstered suite. A single look into Marina's eyes told her that our friend was possessed of demons. For 200 marks she offered us a guaranteed method, tried and tested over the centuries, known as the melon ceremony. To the accompaniment of singing, the patient has a melon strapped to her belly, and has to go to bed for a day and a night with the melon in place. During this time, the sickness moves into the fruit, and if the patient then smashes the melon on the ground, the demon is shattered with it. This all seemed rather too exotic for us, and we made our escape.

The cosy world of magic is just as small as our own. A week later we received a call from a Yugoslavian witch who already knew all about the case. As proof that Marina was bewitched, she suggested that we put a kitchen knife in a saucepan of water, place this under her bed overnight, and take a look at it the next day. If the water was gone, it meant the evil spirit had been in the bedroom and had drunk it. In that case, the knife would have to be thrown out of the window. If it fell tip-first into the earth, Marina would be cured. But as Marina lives on the eleventh floor of a new block and there are always children playing down below, she didn't feel she could start throwing knives out of the window.

By way of an alternative, for a mere 900 marks, the Yugoslavian witch offered a remedy that had never yet been surpassed: Marina would give her a pair of her knickers, and these she would take to Yugoslavia to be blessed by five priests at five different monasteries. Then she would bring the knickers back and Marina would wear them for fourteen days and fourteen nights. Marina's husband would then reappear in two shakes of a lamb's tail. 'But I don't want him to come back,' retorted Marina. 'And anyway, there's a war on in Yugoslavia!' The witch hadn't heard about the war, and we all went home. 'Would she ever have come back with my knickers?' wondered Marina in uncertain tones. I made no reply. For the moment, the wonderful world of magic was over and done with for us.

Suleyman and Salieri

Debates in the media do leave their mark on real life—a minor miracle I recently discovered. The media seize upon a subject, deal with a problem: a reputable paper gives its attention to a reputable problem such as xenophobia and its impact on society, while a less serious-minded paper goes for a less serious-minded subject, say, how to lose weight or something like that. Now the problem needs discussing. That entails at least two fundamentally different views. For example: 'Xenophobia can be combated by reducing the number of foreigners in the country.' Or: 'Xenophobia can be combated by shifting the focus of the hostility felt by the people, and making, say, businessmen rather than foreigners the target.'

The problem of weight loss works in a similar way. You can lose weight in a natural way by eating less, or by other methods, such as liposuction. For a fortnight the subject is debated and then it is thrown out and the next topic takes its place in the paper. Nothing has been solved, but the exchange of views has left its mark: for a while, xenophobia has been a major issue, and suddenly a feeling of camaraderie arises amongst large numbers of people who do not belong together at all and perhaps wanted nothing to do with each other before—Arabs, Jews, Chinese, Turks—all because they have been identified as these very 'foreigners'.

Let's look at an example from everyday life. A Russian theatre, the Nostalgia, was having a go at Pushkin's *Mozart and Salieri*. A friend of mine, an actor from Smolensk, was to play Salieri, the wicked and depressive composer who, motivated by envy and frustration, poisons Mozart at the end of the tragedy. My friend is a harmless fellow, though, married these five years to a Frenchwoman who also acts, and wouldn't hurt a fly. You can tell right away simply by looking at him. The director told him: 'Go right into yourself, deep down, discover the dark side of your soul. There is a criminal in every one of us.' And so on.

My friend, the actor from Smolensk, made a decent effort. He holed up in a bar and went deeper and deeper within himself. After the eighth beer the first signs of an abyss in his soul became apparent, the evil within him welled up, and he became Salieri. In that capacity he did not return to his wife and child, who had been expecting him home for hours and were in despair, but got into his wife's car and, not even having a licence, drove down a one-way street the wrong way, at top speed, in the direction of Wedding. On the way he knocked the wing mirror off a Mercedes. The Mercedes driver gave pursuit and stopped him. As chance would have it, a police patrol car was just passing. For my friend, the actor from Smolensk, the incident could have meant deportation.

'What's your name?' demanded the driver of the Mercedes, a Turk. 'Salieri!' my friend replied. 'Might have guessed—I thought right away you were a foreigner.' Instead of turning to the police for assistance, the Turk took my drunken friend home and was given 100 marks by his wife, the French actress, for everything together: her husband, and the broken mirror, which was really no big deal. Next day the Turk came round again. A friendship developed between them, and the wife's brother, who is French too, now plans to make a film based on the incident.

And so a debate in the media can afford a great many people the opportunity to see each other in a new light, not as Turks or Russians or Ethiopians but as part of the larger community of foreigners in Germany. There is something wonderful about this.

Russian Telephone Sex

There really are a lot of exciting things in Berlin: the new Reichstag and the Soviet memorial, the newborn elephant at Friedrichsfeld zoo, Russian telephone sex numbers. A distorted female voice on tape tries to give succour: 'My friend, I know how lonely you feel in these cruel, unfamiliar streets. Every day you walk streets full of Germans and nobody gives you a smile. Undo your zip and we'll get nostalgic together!'

If I'm being honest, Russian telephone sex has a depressing effect on me. If there were a Turkish telephone sex number in the city too, you could at least make comparisons, and doubtless derive a good deal of valuable sociological insight. The Russian phone sex number is now available to the natives as well: the newspaper *Russkij Berlin* has put a short version in German on the net.

So how does Russian telephone sex differ from the normal German variety?

Firstly, the Russian girls may phone you themselves. On one occasion I taped one such call on my cassette recorder and can now enjoy it any time I like without having to pay DM 3.64 per minute. I can also lend it to friends and acquaintances, free of charge! What's more, I can even work it up as a radio play for Radio MultiKulti, because phone sex calls have no copyright protection.

Now that a number of people have heard the recording, I can vouch for it that Russian telephone sex, and probably the Turkish variety too, has a much greater effect if you do not understand the language. If you don't, then you do not realise how wily Russians really are—in this case, how the girls play a role. Indeed, a large proportion of them are in fact trained actresses.

Yesterday a German theatre director of my acquaintance called to tell me he had just put on a Heiner Müller play at a theatre festival in Chelyabinsk in Siberia.

'We were the sensation of the festival,' he enthused. 'The local papers were beside themselves. I'm going to send the press reviews to the Goethe Institute in Moscow so that they will go on supporting us. But would you mind reading them over before I do, just to be on the safe side? My Russian isn't up to it.' Whereupon he faxed over the text. Even the headline was distinctly curious: 'Six miles aren't too wide a berth for a rabid dog.' The Chelyabinsk theatre critic declared: 'What is behind the glitzy Heiner Müller badge this German company sports? Contempt for the audience, sick self-gratification, or utter bewilderment when faced with present-day reality? The Poles were doped to the eyeballs too, but at least they had more culture.'

Gambling Systems

Vietnamese are passionate players of blackjack, and get royally on the croupiers' nerves. Vietnamese play the Vietnamese system: if they have two cards adding up to 13 or 14 points, they won't take a third, which any superficial Frenchman would take as a matter of course. The Vietnamese are aware that having too many points can only mean losing, and they let the croupier sweat. Probability is on their side, though gambling ethics hereabouts aren't. In this way, however, the Vietnamese win at blackjack. Not for nothing do they all have what's known as the Asian bruise on their thighs, which is said to bode luck at cards. Like the Vietnamese, the Mongols and Chinese have this mark on their thighs too, but they do not play blackjack.

Russians rarely play blackjack, but they often play poker, and enjoy it. To see the players at the only two poker tables in the casino at the Europa Center in Berlin put me in mind of the Politburo in session. Elderly men with moustaches and wearing grey suits cast scathing looks at the Arab in the checked shirt who wasn't playing a consistent game because he had no poker system! Russians win at poker because they do have a system. The Russian system. No matter what cards they happen to hold, they put on a full house expression and exude confidence till the hand is over. Much like the Russian President, who very convincingly used this system to play the never-ageing youngster for years, invariably surrounded by journalists—the main thing being that no one tripped over the extension cable.

At first, superficial Frenchmen reckon the Russians are nuts, but then they concede defeat. They concede! While the men are cleaning out the Arabs at the poker tables, the Russian women are busy losing at roulette. They too have a system: they always bet on a colour, and if they lose they double their stake. Because every Russian woman has taken to heart what Dr Kapiza the Academy professor once said in his TV show 'Incredible But True': 'You can get black three times in a row but never fourteen.'

Red is a different story entirely. Red you can get seventeen times in a row. Russian women are not known for their patience. If the electronic display says it's been black five times in a row, they bet on red right away. In this way Russian women win, but they still go on to lose because they stake all their winnings on some stupid number such as 16, say. Don't ask me why they do it. Maybe because they don't have a mark on their thighs.

When Thai woman play blackjack, everybody else quits. You don't stand a chance if you play blackjack against Thais. I have spent hours watching them play and have tried and tried to figure the Thai system out. I practically dislocated my neck in the process. In vain! What I did establish, with profound admiration, was that the Thai women had committed the entire 72-card sequence to memory within just a few games. This increased the likelihood of their making the right decisions by 100 per cent. With ability of this order, they might long since have been rolling in money, but they don't want to give their secret away. And so, as a precaution, the Thai women always lose it all again.

There are times when the casino in Berlin looks like a special session of the United Nations. I even believe that more nations are represented at the casino than in a routine session of the UN. At every table debates are in progress as to which system works best; the tension rises; the balls spin, the cards are a blur before the eyes. Feeling a little giddy, I take a seat at the bar. Strictly speaking it is only the winners who sit here, those who can break the bank in a single evening. In the end, however, for the fun of it and to preserve their status, they have to lose all their winnings at the tables anyway.

The woman at the bar is called Lisa. She is from England, as is her partner who works as a croupier at the poker table. The employees of the three big Berlin casinos are not allowed to gamble in Berlin. If the management catch them at it, they're out of a job. Lisa told me how hard it is to watch others gambling all day long and not be allowed to do so yourself. She is forever having to resist temptation. It is very trying. In order to relax, the English couple often spend their vacations on Malta, where gaming culture is widely established and you're in for just a quarter-dollar. They trawl the casinos night after night and never go near the beach.

When I asked Lisa about the English system, she shook her head evasively. Once her partner Willy discovered the so-called zero system at roulette. The two of them paid a high price for the discovery—in a single night they gambled their entire holiday funds away. Ever since then, they have been firmly convinced that games of chance are all about chance.

The Turks see things differently and are dedicated players

of the machines. Especially the one-armed bandits, because it is great to pull the lever down. Because Turks have temperament and enjoy sport. The Turkish system goes like this: first they look for a machine that hasn't coughed up a win for a long time. They wait till the witless Frenchman calls it a day, his pockets empty, and then they feed it 5-mark coins till finally it gives up and signals 'check point' to the accompaniment of music and flashing lights. With this system you mustn't ever be economical or insert anything under a 5-mark coin, or you won't get your 'check point'.

The Germans shove their oar in everywhere, without any system. They play poker, they gad about the blackjack tables, they pull down the levers on the machines, and they follow the ball as it spins round the roulette dish. If they win they do not rejoice, and if they lose they remain indifferent. Essentially they aren't there for the gambling. The Germans go to the casino because they have an open mind about the ways of the world and are curious. There they get acquainted with the systems of other countries, which when all's said and done don't interest them particularly.

On one occasion, it was long past midnight, the lights went out in the casino. All the systems were confounded; the gamblers of all the nations cursed, each in his own language. It sounded like the very last day of Babylon. At that moment I realised that every single one of them, no matter what their differences, wanted one and the same thing: for the power to come back on.

No Flies in Berlin

To me, Berlin seems like a health resort. Firstly, because of the mild weather. In summer it is rarely too hot, in winter it's never really cold. And what's more, there aren't many flies at all, and here in Prenzlauer Berg there are none at all. In New York the mosquitoes are a traffic hazard, they spread disease, virtually seeing to it that epidemics are constantly plaguing the city. In Moscow too the problem of flies is an ongoing one. When I was there recently I saw a TV newscaster reading the late news suddenly slap himself on the face, and I also saw homeless people in the streets making soup out of flies. Everywhere in the world there are flies. Only here are there none. Of course that isn't the only reason why I like Berlin so much. To my mind, the people are cool. Most of those who live in the capital are calm, composed and contemplative. And just think what has happened in recent years: the Wall fell, Germany was reunified, the casino in the Europa Center closed its doors. In spite of it all, few ever lose it completely. Berliners always do what they think is right, and they enjoy life. In Moscow, by contrast, there was a whole run of suicides when on one occasion the evening news was broadcast twenty minutes late, and many fled the city, thinking the end of the world was nigh. Statistics show that in Russia only 17.8 per cent of the population enjoy life. Too many flies, probably. Which is why I prefer Berlin.

Not long ago in Schönhauser Allee I bumped into my neighbour, the Vietnamese man who keeps the greengrocer's. He's had a perm. His approach to cultural integration. Now he looks like Paganini. 'You're a regular Paganini, Chack!' I told him. 'A Paganini!' 'Sorry, I'm clean out of it,' he said 'but zucchini I do have, see right here.' There we both are in Schönhauser Allee, him with a perm on his head and a zucchini in his hand, me beside him. Where are the Japanese tourists with their expensive cameras? They're probably stuck in a traffic jam: not every tour coach manages even half of Schönhauser Allee.

Of course Berlin has its flaws as well. The Nazis, for instance. Two weeks ago the Republicans held a campaign event on Schönhauser Allee. A huge election poster read 'Telling them what's what' and below it two lads were handing out flyers. 'Pretty Woman' was coming from the loudspeaker. 'Step right up and we'll show you something,' one of the youngsters was saying to passers-by. The passers-by for their part kept their distance. In German the slogan read 'Mal zeigen, was 'ne Harke ist'—literally, 'Showing them what a mattock is'—and people were probably afraid of this mysterious mattock. Myself, I didn't exactly know what a mattock was, so I asked two elderly women beside me. 'A mattock? Well, it's like a spade, I'd say, only pointed,' one of the women answered. 'For gardening.' 'More for grave-digging,' responded the other. 'I'll bear it in mind,' I said. 'Oh, you needn't bother, it isn't a good word. That's how they are, our Nazis, always thinking up some new nonsense,' the two women told me comfortingly. I went home. Wherever you may be there is someone who wants to tell you what's what, or show you what a mattock is, be it in Russia, America or Vietnam. But at least there are no flies in Berlin.

Jump out of the Window

The German law on asylum is as capricious as a woman whose reasons for preference or rejection are beyond comprehension. With one asylum seeker, the law falls in love at first sight, and won't let him go. The next, it kicks up the arse. A short while ago in Schönhauser Allee I met an old acquaintance who had evidently been out of luck with asylum law. He had already tried twice to get on the good side of the law, but he was invariably deported. Anyone else would have given up long since, but he hadn't abandoned hope, and both times he sneaked back into the country illegally through the back door.

Now there he was walking about town with one leg in plaster. I asked him what had happened, and he told me the dramatic story of the most recent time he was arrested. He was driving down Greifswalder Strasse on his way to the Obi DIY centre. The police stopped him because he wasn't wearing his seat belt. Checking his papers, they found to their delight that he was one of the many men long wanted for deportation. So he ended up in a cell, waiting to be deported. He knew the rules: before an illegal immigrant could be deported, he was given the opportunity to return to the place he had last resided and pack his belongings. A friend visited him in jail and brought him a few little essentials. As they were parting, the friend whispered to him: 'Jump out of the window.'

The following day, when my acquaintance was taken by two policemen to his flat in Greifswalder Strasse, where they removed his handcuffs, he took his friend's advice and jumped out of the second-floor window. His friend hadn't been spinning him a line. He really was waiting down below, and had made all the necessary preparations to catch him. But he was standing beneath the wrong window. And in any case, my acquaintance misjudged the distance, jumped too far out, and smashed right into a street lamp. Luckily he was able to grab hold of an NPD poster reading 'Mut zur Wahl-wähle National'—take courage and vote for the National Party. Together with the poster he slid slowly to the ground. His friend yanked him into the car. They left the NPD poster behind. A few hours later my acquaintance realised that his leg was swelling up steadily. He went to see the 'surgeon', a Russian doctor in illegal practice, who cured illegal patients of legal ailments. The 'surgeon' examined him and diagnosed a broken leg. Now my acquaintance will have his leg in plaster for a month, and will have to forget about driving entirely for the moment.

'One thing I did learn from the whole business,' he told me, taking a good drag on my cigarette. 'Always fasten your seat belt!'

A Lost Day

A newspaper arts editor calls me up. He wants something, anything at all, on youth culture. At 10 a.m., for heaven's sake. What on earth is it anyway, youth culture? I phone my friend Kolia, who always knows where it's at. He suggests maybe I should watch MTV. The more I watch it, the better. They start at eight, I've already missed the intros. So what. I turn on the TV: fat black men are dancing round a tree. The phone rings. It is one Herr Kravchuck, a reporter from *Spiegel spezial*, complaining that for a feature he is doing on eastern European intellectuals living in Berlin he has been able to locate next to no suitable candidates. The only Russians he has found are elderly, frustrated types, and he has not managed to track down any Bulgarians at all. This gets me het up. What? No Bulgarians? But they're everywhere. You just don't spot them because they do such a perfect impression of the Germans. Every orchestra in Germany has a Bulgarian conductor, the professors at the universities are mainly Bulgarian, and then there's the winner of the Stockhausen Prize, and, finally, there's the Bulgarian Cultural Institute. And if we're talking eastern European intellectuals, then, dammit, there's me too.

The man from the *Spiegel* writes it all down and agrees that I absolutely have to be in the special feature.

'The photographer will be round in twenty minutes to take some pictures of you.' Hastily I pull on some trousers and look out a clean shirt. Meanwhile I keep an eye on MTV, in pursuit of youth culture. The fat black men are still circling their tree, undeterred. The photographer's name is Karsten and he wants to photograph me in a crowd, the favourite cliché when it comes to portraying an eastern European intellectual: a stranger, but somehow just like you and me. I have to stroll up and down Schönhauser Allee twenty-three times. And it still isn't working out right. The crowd instantly spot the man with the camera, and scatter in every direction. In the end, Karsten changes his tactics. He hides in the crowd himself and waits for a good moment. While he's at it, his mobile phone is stolen. Two hours later I'm back home again. On TV, Beavis and Butthead are going to the cinema. Ok, boys, I'm back, let's move it here, let's have some youth culture. Me and Beavis and Butthead watch a video clip featuring the band Prodigy. Something has happened to a case, it tumbles down to the river and eight perspiring men go running after it. Then they all fall into the river and that is the end of the story. The fat black men go on with their circuits of the tree. One of them is bleeding. 'Why is he leaping around like that?' asks Butthead. 'Beats me,' says Beavis. 'Maybe someone shoved the *Spiegel spezial* feature on eastern European intellectuals up his arse. HA HA HA! And set fire to it. HEH HEH HEH!'

The phone rings. The editor of the Russian section at Radio MultiKulti says that this evening at the Arsenal Cinema they're showing the first Soviet science-fiction film, *Aelita*, made in 1924. He wants me to write a piece on it, and insists that he wants original sound on tape. The recorder and a microphone are ready and waiting for me at SFB Radio, I just have to pick them up.

I spend the forty-five minutes of the underground train ride thinking about youth culture. The result is zilch. How annoying. I have nothing whatsoever to say on the subject. The lad across from me is flipping through a magazine and grinning. That is it! Youth culture! I sit down beside him and ask what he's reading. It's an IKEA catalogue.

Right, I've picked up the gear, everything is ready. The film starts at 7 p.m. At ten to seven I am already in the auditorium. I take a seat in the third row, squarely across from the huge loudspeaker, and prepare everything for the recording. At seven the film begins. It is about a revolution on Mars. The ruler of Mars, armed with a glass knife, pursues a young woman with a wobbly backside. The woman opens her mouth. At this point, screams for help ought to be coming from that mouth, but I am holding the microphone in vain. The film is absolutely soundless. Silent. As silent as only a Russian silent movie made in 1924 can be.

An embarrassing situation. A graveyard silence prevails in the cinema. I gather up my things and pick my way out carefully, microphone in hand. In the foyer, the cinema staff have a good laugh at my expense. They might at least have behaved as if nothing had happened. It's not as if they get a radio journalist at a silent movie screening every day.

On the way home I carry on thinking about youth culture. To my eyes, the youngsters in the subway all look like Beavis and Butthead. Back home I turn on MTV. Björk is pointing her finger at a fat book. The running text on screen reads: 'Björk learned to read especially for this video.' Three literary editors worked with Björk for three months. A great achievement. I call the newspaper arts editor and ask him to be more specific in his brief. Does he want a serious examination of youth culture? Crap! He meant Jewish culture, Judenkultur, not youth culture, Jugendkultur. The best thing I can do now is go out for a drink. It has been a lost day.

The Woman Who Gives Life to Everyone

Our friend Katja is a devotee of the great drug mystic Carlos Castaneda. She has read all the books by him that she could get hold of, she bought mescalin cacti, and she even bought a special lamp burner for 160 marks. She frequently attended secret gatherings where she and other Castaneda fans shared spiritual experiences. In fact she went to quite a lot. Before very long, she could separate her conscious from her subconscious and her body from her mind without much effort at all. Thus Katja achieved ongoing access to the astral plane, where she met numerous interesting personalities, among them Castaneda himself.

Things were going famously till one day her mind and body were unable to rejoin each other and were checked in separately to the psychiatric station at the Queen Elisabeth Herzberg Clinic in Lichtenberg. There, with the assistance of modern medicine (including 'drum-kit therapy'), Katja was reassembled. Her health returned to normal, but she was forbidden access to the astral realm.

Under medical supervision, Katja fundamentally rethought her life and arrived at the conviction that her great task was to bring new life into the world. She began in a modest way, with dogs. Her husband, a not especially successful businessman, had been unlucky with a new business idea. He had hoped to get rich by selling drinks at the Love Parade, but some villains assigned him a location for his stand on the wrong street. All day long he waited in vain for thirsty ravers, but all he got was an old woman who took pity on him as she passed and bought a warm iced lemonade. So there he sat, wretched, with sixty crates of beer and lemonade and not a clue how to get rid of them. Katja talked him into borrowing more money and buying a pair of Shar-Pei dogs. Breeding these pedigree Chinese dogs would earn back all the money they'd lost.

Just five months later, five cute whelps were running about the flat. The Shar-Pei dogs required special care. Their eyelids had to be continually shaved and they weren't allowed to run down the stairs because, with their big heads and little backsides, they instantly tipped over. Katja looked after them day and night, but did not manage to sell a single one. Once all five had grown into huge full-sized dogs, Katja lost interest in them. She partitioned the flat with iron bars and wire mesh: one part, including the bathroom, the dogs took over, while in the other part Katja devoted herself to the plants she had now bought. She achieved the impossible: within six months, her room looked like a jungle. The songbirds that came with the jungle, however, never had time to acclimatise: they were the victims of a surprise attack by the Shar-Pei dogs.

To introduce new life into her domestic jungle, Katja decided to have children. It proved a long struggle. On the one hand, with her doctors; she even took one to court because he had expressed doubts about her ability to conceive. On the other, with her own husband, though in fact he no longer dared set foot in the flat, and hadn't been to the toilet for a year. Katja took every hurdle with bravura. Now two little ones are already growing up in Katja's jungle, two girls: Deborah and Susann. If they should ever succeed in reaching adulthood, they will doubtless possess many a practical accomplishment in life. Tarzan and Jane would hang themselves on the nearest creeper out of sheer envy and resentment.

Business Camouflage

One day, I chanced to venture forth as far as Wilmersdorf. I wanted to show my friend Ilia Kitup, a poet from Moscow, some typical nooks of Berlin.

It was already midnight, we were hungry, and we ended up in a Turkish snack bar. The two men who worked there evidently had nothing to do and were placidly drinking their tea.

The music from the speakers sounded familiar to my friend. He recognised the voice of a famous Bulgarian female singer and sang along with a couple of verses.

'Do the Turks always listen to Bulgarian music at night?' I asked Kitup, who studied anthropology in Moscow and is thoroughly familiar with the ways of these people. He got into a conversation with the two men at the counter.

'They aren't Turks, they're Bulgarians pretending to be Turks,' explained Kitup, who had a little Bulgarian blood in his own veins too. 'It's probably their business camouflage.' 'But why should they do that?' I asked. 'Berlin is already too diverse,' the men told us. 'There's no point in complicating the situation unnecessarily. The consumer is used to being served by Turks at a Turkish snack bar, even if they're really Bulgarians.'

The very next day I went to a Bulgarian restaurant I had recently discovered. I had a notion that the Bulgarians there were really Turks, but they turned out to be the genuine Bulgarian article. The Italians in the Italian restaurant next door, however, proved to be Greek. They had taken over the restaurant and then signed on for evening classes in Italian, they told me. When you go to an Italian restaurant, you at least expect the staff to talk a bit of Italian to you. A little later I went to a Greek restaurant. My instinct was spot on: the staff turned out to be Arabs.

Berlin is a mysterious city. Nothing is as it first appears. In the sushi bar in Oranienburger Strasse there was a girl from the Buryat Republic behind the counter. From her I learned that most sushi bars in Berlin are in the ownership of Jews, who have arrived here not from Japan but from America. This is not unusual in the gastronomic field. Just as cheap tinned carrots from the Aldi supermarket are served up as hand-trimmed Gascony fruits of the earth, the principle remains that nothing is the real thing here, and everyone is at the same time himself and someone else.

I remained on the trail and continued my investigations. Every day I learned more. The Chinese at the snack bar across from my house are Vietnamese. The Indian in Rykestrasse is in reality a Tunisian of conviction, from Carthage. And the man who runs the Afro-American bar with all the voodoo stuff on the walls is—a Belgian.

Even those last bulwarks of authenticity, the Vietnamese cigarette vendors, are little more than a cliché created by television series and police crackdowns. But still, everyone involved maintains the illusion, even though every policeman knows that most of these so-called Vietnamese are from Inner Mongolia.

I was extremely surprised by what my investigations had brought to light, and continued them all around the city, in quest of the last remaining unfaked truth. Above all, I wanted to know who the people known as Germans really are, the ones who run those typical German restaurants that serve knuckle of pork with sauerkraut, those little cosy pubs called Olly's or Scholly's or some such, where the beer always costs half what it costs elsewhere. But there I encountered a wall of silence. My instinct tells me I am on the track of a big story. But I cannot get any further with it on my own. If anyone can really say what lies concealed behind the attractive façade of a 'German' pub, do please get in touch. I'd be grateful for any help.

The Turkish Tom-Cat

One day our Turkish tom-cat disappeared as suddenly as he had appeared, seven years previously, in our Wedding backyard. Back then it was my wife who discovered him on our steps. For two days he sat out there on the staircase and never moved from the spot. He was big and black and had two white paws. We adopted him right away and named him Masja. Masja turned his nose up at every brand of cat food. All he would eat was Turkish foods such as kebab and round flat Turkish bread. From this we concluded that he had previously been kept by a Turkish family. Every attempt to integrate the tom into our society failed. Instead of heightening the cosiness of our flat, he was forever causing stress and chaos. Masja behaved like a real macho—he came and went as he pleased, would hardly ever consent to be stroked, and tore to and fro around the flat like one possessed. Whenever he missed the door and slammed into the wall, he pretended it was exactly what he had meant to do. On Fridays he always crapped in the bathtub. He had made our bathtub his mosque.

In the yard, Masja got into a complicated situation. He started an affair with an older cat who could have been his mother. She became pregnant and produced a litter of five. Masja took up with one of the kittens: she was his lover, sister and daughter all in one. She grew apace, and soon the day would be coming when she too would be a mother. To avoid any further escalation of incest in our yard, I decided to have Masja neutered. He suspected what I was planning and went into hiding. On Friday we were waiting for him by his bathroom mosque. When he turned up there, punctual as ever, I bundled him into a big holdall and took him to the vet. Masja was given a ketamine injection and his eyes glazed over like two 2-mark coins.

At lightning speed the doctor removed his testicles. 'You clearly know what you're doing,' I told him enthusiastically. 'That'll be 100 marks,' he replied. I was hoping the operation would enable Masja to make a new start: once castrated, he might find it easier to adapt to our company? 'Balls off, tolerance up,' I thought. Masja spent the next two days on a ketamine trip. Once his eyes returned to normal, he went out into the yard—and never came back.

For a whole month we waited for him. Then we decided to get a new pet. This time we would have something exotic. I leafed through the weekly paper, *Russkij Berlin*, and found three ads which I took to be offering pets: 'Female boxer, bad parents, seeks new home,' 'Snow-white Persian (tom) seeks girlfriend for intimate moments,' 'Good home sought for Russian chinchilla'. We didn't want the bad female. The snow-white Persian turned out to be human and merely happened to have been born in the year of the tom-cat according to the Chinese calendar. That left the chinchilla, which we ended up buying for 50 marks. We called him Dusja. He now lives with us, in a cage. He likes to chew up books and telephone cables, takes his bath in special chinchilla sand, and has a whole variety of exotic ways. Even so, I have a suspicion that in reality he is simply a Russian squirrel.

The Russian Mafia Joint

My friend and namesake Wladimir from Vilnius is a shy person. In particular, he suffers from the prospect of having to talk about his future with the Nice Lady at the welfare office when he makes his obligatory visit. Every time the woman assigned to his case stings him, wasp-like, with observations such as 'Spare a thought for your future' or 'You can't live on welfare for ever', Wladimir blushes, stares at the floor and remains as silent as a partisan captured by the Gestapo. Only once, when the Nice Lady went too far and began to doubt his manhood, did my friend lose his self-control and confess his long-held dream to her: that he would really like to be a major-league businessman and could easily see himself with a future as a restaurant proprietor.

'Aha!' The Nice Lady was thrilled: 'Dipping a toe in the waters of self-employment! Exactly what we're after! It's not easy, but we shall give you all the support we can,' she said, and referred Wladimir to a retraining opportunity, 'Businessman 2000: foreign trade on an east-west basis', which had been especially set up and funded by the Berlin Senate for the benefit of foreign nationals on welfare.

At BIBIZ (which means 'prick' in Lithuanian but in German stands for the Berliner Informations- und Bildungs-Zentrum, the Berlin Information and Education Centre) Wladimir embarked on his studies alongside other future businessmen and women. His group consisted of two elderly Bulgarian ladies, three Vietnamese and a fat girl from the Caribbean. For six months they chewed over the ABC of business: economics, electronic data processing, business English, etc. When it was over, Wladimir got a diploma and made an appearance once again, in his new capacity as a Businessman 2000, in the Nice Lady's office. He now had almost all the prerequisites he needed to make his dream come true—the necessary know-how, a powerful will to succeed, and even an EU driving licence. All he lacked was the money. Because without money there is no east-west trade.

Before long he was off again, like it or not, collecting written confirmation from tobacconists or newsagents, to the effect that his services were not required. As luck would have it, just then his mother had a pension approved by the Federal Insurance Agency, one she had applied for three years previously. With this substantial sum, Wladimir paid the deposit on a Turkish snack bar that had just gone out of business in a nearby side-street. There he hoped to make the dream of a restaurant of his own come true. He did all the renovation work himself and painted abstract art on the walls and the tiled floor.

'If a business is to win over the hearts of its customers, it has to make an impact, in every respect,' he declared when I visited him at his bar shortly before it opened. 'We'll do international cuisine: German, Chinese, Italian, French...' 'And who is going to cook it all?' I asked him. 'Me!' the Businessman 2000 pronounced, and stared at the floor. 'Basically it isn't so very complicated. All you need are the right sauces.' His resolve convinced me that Wladimir would always come up with the right sauce. 'We are aiming at a young, international clientele, and of course tourists as well, since they can't get this kind of thing anywhere else.' At that moment a woman of about eighty came into the bar and asked for the lavatory. Even this customer request enchanted Wladimir: 'There you have it,' he informed me when she had gone. 'Our position is strategically very good. I'm planning to convert the toilets soon too.'

My friend has an unshakeable belief that his business will see him into twenty-first century success. The only problem is that he hasn't found the right name for it yet. The regulars at the Jägermeister bar across the road have long since hit on a nickname for his place, though: the Russian mafia joint.

No More Trips to Weimar

At the invitation of the Thuringian Literary Society, I paid the first visit of my life to Weimar, to take part in a festival called 'Eastern Europe in Times of Change: Revolution and Counter-Revolution', together with two dozen other eastern European artists: Poles, Russians, Czechs and Ukrainians. In the course of it, it emerged just how different our times of change had been. Our group proved a pretty poisonous mixture. Only the warm Ukrainian vodka ensured a modicum of tolerance.

The German culture capital looked like a wedge of cream gateau in a microwave, or a huge exhibition just being opened. Though it was 37°C in the shade, in three days we viewed everything the culture capital had to offer: the freshly painted dorms and restored crematoria of Buchenwald concentration camp; the dusty coffins of Schiller and Goethe, which could also be seen if you paid 10 marks entrance, and likewise their various houses; Hitler's private art collection, the Nietzsche archive, and the bee museum, as well as an exhibition to mark the jubilee of the Weimaraner, the breed of pointer Thuringia is so proud of. The tourist hordes were everywhere, in every pub there was a Goethe Room, in every lavatory a memorial plaque. We chased from one exhibition to another and in between, of course, we made our own appearances. The rest of the time we passed discussing art. The three Russians I met were particularly drawn to Anselm Kiefer, some of whose pictures hung in the Weimar Museum of Modern Art. The Russians asked me where the artist was now and what he was doing. I had no idea; all I was familiar with was his activity during the early Occupation, when he toured the German provinces wearing an SS uniform, conquering one small town after another. With a photographer trailing him all the time, needless to say. His pictures did not fetch really high prices until the Americans began to take an interest. They bought a lot of his works, *Morning Sunlight on the Führer's Table* and suchlike.

The women and the eagles in the Hitler collection went down well with us too. If I had enough room in my flat, and enough money, I'd hang a collection of women like that in my place: women nude and semi-nude, girls with flowers, girls without flowers. The sense of power: every little miss in the whole wide world is mine, all mine. Otherwise the collection was highly eclectic. My Russian friends stopped in front of one portrait: an old red-nosed man with the swollen eyes of a drinker. Whatever had got into the Führer when he acquired this old fellow? After all, the eagles, women, sportsmen, landscapes, factories, can all be understood as aspects of the Nazi aesthetic, or something like that. But this old soak? Perhaps Hitler had been strolling along a seaside promenade in a cheerful mood, the sun was shining, and everything was going nicely. Then his eye fell upon this poor artist, the wretched picture, and he thought: 'What the hell, I'll buy this old so-and-so and give the lad a break.' 'The same thing's happened to me too,' said one of the Russian artists. 'What makes you think he actually bought this garbage?' retorted one of the others. 'He'll have been given it as a present, for sure, by some comrade in the party. Some guy comes over and says: "Say, Adolf, I've been doing a bit of painting. You understand these things. What do you think of it?" Hitler looks at the old fellow in the picture. "Very interesting," he says. "You feel this is life. You still have a lot to learn, though." The painter thinks Hitler is telling the truth and he's delighted: "You know, Adolf, if you like it so much, it's yours. Hang it in your study. It'll bring you luck."' The third Russian puts in, 'That's just how it was with me and Andreyev. Every time he stops by at our place he races off to my studio like a lunatic to see if his crap installation is still in place. Artists often enslave their friends.'

We strolled back to the Kiefer exhibition to look at Operation Sea Lion a fourth time. The Russians were arguing. 'These are the Germans, those are the British!' 'No, it's the other way round!' But Edvard Munch was good too. My attempt to buy a new pair of socks in Weimar failed. Then the festival was over.

On the return journey the artists' train, the 'Caspar David Friedrich', stopped just before Merseburg. The overhead wires had melted and fallen down. The outside temperature was 38°C. From the window we could see the Karl von Basedow Hospital. The air conditioning stopped working. After ten minutes of this, two ambulances took the first victims off to the hospital; after half an hour the bar on the train had been drunk dry. The German passengers were queuing at the only card-phone, but the rate was so exorbitant that the phonecards were rapidly used up. Before long the phone gave up the ghost entirely. Deutsche Bahn's perspiring incidents manager went round handing out 50-mark vouchers. The prevailing mood suddenly improved. A gang of schoolkids took over the restaurant car.

Once the next casualties were on their way to the Karl von Basedow Hospital, a debate started up among the passengers. A bald theologian spoke in defence of the Pope. An elderly lady assumed the role of the intellectual in despair: 'I'm Protestant,' she said, 'but after everything that's happened to us Germans, the whole concept of religion needs fundamentally rethinking.' Old Baldie insisted that the actions of the Vatican could not be explained by human logic. The youngsters adopted the most radical position: 'We'll jettison everything!' They enjoyed the talk-show quality of the restaurant car debate enormously. 'I'm a Protestant atheist,' one girl confessed. 'My parents even had me properly transformed in the church.' 'I'm a Protestant Catholic,' another girl claimed; 'so I say, no sex before marriage.' 'Come off it,' her fifteen-year-old boyfriend griped, 'you're not exactly Mother Teresa.' You'd never get a discussion like that in a moving train. Only if it's stopped. 'Whenever man feels he's lacking something, he remembers God,' the theologian declared proudly.

Two hours later the power came back on and we continued our journey. Weimar was left behind us, and God we left somewhere near Merseburg.

Nuts from Around the World and German Mushrooms from Saxony

Berlin is not exactly the city of the poor, but here as elsewhere there are increasingly disadvantaged sections of the population: students reading humanities subjects, single mothers, or street musicians with drug addictions. Not until you have completed your studies are you entitled to welfare. So graduates in theology are more often to be found talking to the social security office than to God. Even a student who is getting a grant of 800 marks a month, half of it needed for his rent, would be vegetating below the welfare level if it weren't for student jobs. But then, what jobs does a prospective humanities graduate get offered by the student job exchange? My friend Sasha from the Ukraine, who has been reading Slavic studies at the Humboldt University for two years, had a choice between dish-washing in an Australian crocodile steakhouse, cleaning the lavatories in the Beate Uhse Museum of Erotica, or helping with liposuction treatment at a beauty clinic. Though he is himself a vegetarian, Sasha opted for the crocodile restaurant, and was revolted from morning till night. Fortunately it was not long before he got to know Unter Wasser, a Russian rock bank who also ran a removals service, and he went to work for them as a furniture loader.

Working in the removals sector strengthens a man's muscles and broadens his mental horizon. Every day you're meeting new people, entering new apartments, and making contacts. On one occasion, Sasha helped two women with their move. They ran a stand on Winterfeldplatz which bore the delightful legend Nuts from around the World and German Mushrooms from Saxony. The two women, who were raising a child together, took a liking to Sasha and promptly gave him a job as a vendor on the stand. Effortlessly he transferred from removals to selling nuts.

At first he found the business a little weird. One of the women, Melina, was Greek and responsible for the nuts from around the world, while the other, Sabine from Saxony, supplied the mushrooms. She fetched them from her home area by car. Where the nuts from around the world were procured remained a secret. They came in large sacks and had to be sorted in the store. To do this work, the two women had taken on several members of Papa Karlo, a Siberian rock band. In order to make a success of selling the nuts, Sasha had to learn worldwide nut geography by heart. Customers hankering after knowledge wanted to know everything when they shopped at the stand on Winterfeldplatz. 'Where are these walnuts from?' one would ask. 'France,' answered Sasha. 'And the macadamias?' 'California?' 'And the Brazil nuts?' 'A special offer from Pakistan.' 'And where do you come from?' 'I'm from the southern Ukraine,' said honest Sasha. 'Aha!' the customer would say in astonishment, trying to establish a connection between the produce and the vendor. But it defeated his imagination. Another customer thought it was a genuinely multicultural venture and bought an entire kilogram of pumpkin seeds.

At first, Sasha was not allowed to work more than two days a week on the stand. But now the women are having a second child, and during their maternity leave he will be running the business.

An unusual career for a man reading Slavic studies in Berlin.

The Professor

When the professor came to Germany he had a good deal more money than the average immigrant. He never even considered a life on welfare. On the contrary, the professor bought himself a Ford Scorpio right away, and in no time at all, with the help of an estate agent, he had bought a large, light flat in Knaackstrasse. At the Krupskaya Pedagogical Institute in Moscow the professor had taught 'The Education of Young People in Socialist Society'. He had additionally done research into the role of various domestic animals in village folklore.

The scholarly work which had earned him the title of professor and had subsequently been published in book form was entitled 'The Significance of the Goat in the Mentality of the Russian People'. Although he was a member of the Communist Party of the Soviet Union, the professor held no clearly defined political views. That is to say, he did have some, but he didn't really. At times he gave thought to ways in which everything in the country might be better organised, but he never wrote his thoughts down, nor did he confide them to anyone. Like many of his contemporaries, the professor was a liberal. When the end came for socialism and the new era dawned, the professor failed to perceive immediately the dangers inherent in such a change. Naively, the good fellow supposed he would be perfectly well able to carry on teaching 'The Education of Young People in Capitalist Society'. But things turned out differently. Nobody required such tuition any more; young people took their education into their own hands, and the Institute was closed. The premises were rented out to the promoter of a techno club. The professor's salary was paid more and more irregularly, and at length ceased altogether. The government was unable to pay all the employees who were now suddenly out of work. 'First the miners,' said a government spokesman on TV, 'then the doctors.'

At first the unemployed professor watched a lot of television. It seemed to him the way to decipher the cryptic messages of the new era. He took a particular interest in the new programme 'What's To Be Done', which was aimed at the Russian intelligentsia and had few commercials. The message was not easy to interpret, however. 'Go into the woods,' the presenter advised, 'and gather the mushrooms and berries.' 'Go into the woods yourself!' the professor snapped back blithely and switched off. His liberal friends maintained that the only solution was to emigrate. The professor packed his belongings, sold his flat and moved to Germany. There, being half Jewish, he was granted asylum and given permission to remain. One thing only tormented him: he had nothing to do.

In the Russian newspaper he noticed an advertisement seeking child-minders for a Russian kindergarten that was being established in Berlin. The professor promptly applied for a job. The two young women who ran the kindergarten hired him at 9 marks an hour. In the evenings he went round to his neighbour, a tailor who also came from Russia and was in fact an archaeologist by training. Not until he arrived in Germany, where there was not so much to be dug up, did he retrain. These days the archaeologist went to flea markets to buy cheap garments which he would take apart and sew into new, chic clothes which he sold in a Russian boutique on Kurfürstendamm. Every evening he sat at his sewing machine and the professor would tell him the story of his messed-up life.

At first the archaeologist listened with interest, but at some point he realised that the professor often repeated himself, and furthermore his stories distracted him so much that he was unable to sew properly. 'You know what, my friend,' he told the professor one day, 'these stories are all so superb, you really ought to write them down. It could be a terrific novel. I know a man who publishes books in Russian here and I'd be glad to recommend you to him.' The professor liked the idea. It restored meaning to his life.

For months on end he was locked away in his study. One day in spring he reappeared at the tailor's holding a stout leather briefcase. Proudly he pulled forth a thick sheaf of paper. 'Here it is,' he said, 'my novel. Do read it quickly, please, but read it carefully. I'll leave the bag with you so that none of the pages go astray. I'd be greatly interested in your opinion.' With that he left. The tailor tossed the manuscript in the bin. After all, he'd heard all the stories before. But he unpicked the professor's old leather briefcase and sewed himself a pair of swimming trunks. This was a long-held dream come true. Once, back in the days when he was studying archaeology in the Soviet Union, he had received a letter from America. His aunt, who had been living there for twenty years, was planning to visit Russia and enquired what he might like in the way of gifts. He had no particularly clear recollection of his aunt, and was leading a decidedly impoverished student life. He needed everything. He had neither a proper place to live nor enough to eat. Full of bitterness, he wrote back saying that, thank you, he had all he wanted, the only thing he didn't have was a pair of leather swimming trunks, which he'd be very glad of. His aunt didn't get the joke. When she arrived in Moscow she had a whole trunk of presents with her, but no swimming trunks. 'I'm so sorry, my boy,' she said. 'I combed all America but I couldn't find leather swimming trunks anywhere. I guess they're out of fashion in our parts.' Wherever his fate took him in later years, the tailor always remembered that story. Now he had them—his crazy swimming trunks made from the professor's briefcase.

Once a week the professor tentatively enquired if the tailor had read his novel yet. 'I've been so busy,' the tailor responded every time, with an eloquent shake of the head. But the professor didn't give up. One Sunday he turned up early in the morning. It was already summer by now, and the tailor was sitting on his balcony with a bottle of beer in hand, enjoying the sun. He was wearing only a pair of swimming trunks— the leather ones. The professor sat down beside him and helped himself to a bottle of Berliner Pilsner as well. 'Oh, by the way,' he began, 'have you had a chance to read any of my manuscript?' 'I have indeed,' replied the tailor. 'It's most impressive, to my mind, the way you describe it all.' The professor's eye was caught by the shorts the other was wearing. 'A new creation? Funny thing, I used to have a briefcase that was that very colour.' 'Nonsense,' said the tailor, 'I know what your briefcase looks like. It's quite different.' 'Different?' 'Yes, quite different!'

The sun beamed.

My Little Friend

The love of foreign languages can cost you dearly. My friend Klaus has been in a Russian prison for a month, and all he wanted to do was learn Russian. In Berlin he was always listening to 'Deutsche Welle', the Russian language learning programme targeted at children from five to ten years old. Twice a week, for a whole year. The upshot was that he began every sentence with 'And now, my little friend.' He wouldn't even have managed in a kindergarten. Klaus was in urgent need of someone to talk Russian to. I didn't have the time and recommended placing an ad in *Tip und Zitty*—'Bed for rent, suit Russian emigrants' or something of the sort. It wasn't long before the first Russian, Sergei, got in touch with him.

He had come to Germany a year before, in an artists' exchange programme. For six months he had represented contemporary Russian art at the Bethany Artists' House. Then the exchange was at an end. But Sergei did not want to leave Berlin, and decided to remain illegally. By day he worked on a building site, and in the evenings he indulged his passion, eating snails bought from the food department of the KDW department store. A hobby that cost him almost every pfennig he earned. At first Sergei was living in one of the houses at Friedrichshain that squatters had occupied. When the police cleared the squatters out, he managed to make his getaway at the last moment. So then Klaus put a bed in the corner of his one-room apartment for Sergei. 'And now, my little friend,' he would say every day, 'you must help me improve my Russian.' But it didn't really work. The two of them were too different, and the apartment was too small. Klaus, a vegetarian by conviction, had to put up with Sergei's revolting eating habits day in, day out. On one occasion he made a secret bid to save some of the giant snails, rescuing them from the bowl under Sergei's bed and hiding them in the cupboard.

One day Sergei made his landlord an offer. How about he move to Moscow for a week or so and stay with Sergei's wife, and improve his Russian there?

Klaus got himself a visa right away and flew to Moscow. Sergei's wife was called Mila, and she knew nothing about the story. She had a small room in a council flat. There was no telephone, and five other families were living there too. It was a very lively flat, with three gas stoves in the kitchen, one toilet, and a lot of screaming children in the corridor. But when Klaus arrived, it seemed almost deserted. An old woman who lived there had just died, the pool attendant who lived on his own had been arrested for theft, and the children were on holiday with their parents.

The only person who was at home when Klaus showed up was a policeman, the jealous lover of Sergei's wife. 'Good day! I'm from Germany. And now, my little friend, show me where Mila lives,' Klaus said to him. The man made no reply. He let the visitor in, showed him Mila's room, and vanished into his own. Klaus, who was tired after his long journey, soon fell asleep.

That evening Mila came home from the library where she worked and went straight to her lover's room. Next morning, the two of them had quarrelled about Mila's husband, AWOL somewhere in Germany. The policeman thought Klaus was a rival, and that evening, when Mila entered his room, he started up with more accusations. The quarrel became so violent that the policeman ended up fetching an axe and killing Mila. Then he locked the door from the outside and scarpered. Klaus spent two days on his own in the unfamiliar room, till in the end he noticed blood on the floor. It had seeped through the thin partition wall from the next room. Klaus opened the window and yelled: 'Blood on the floor, my little friends, blood on the floor!' 'Another nutcase,' muttered an old woman who was collecting empty bottles in the courtyard. But just in case, she called the police. They assumed Klaus to be the murderer, and naturally didn't buy the story about a language-learning trip. Despite having a German passport, he was locked up. While he was in prison awaiting trial, the other inmates gave him a nickname: the blood-on-the-floor man.

The Birch Woman

The day has arrived—Markus Lenz has his picture in the paper. When I first met him, Markus was a passionate collector. Two things chiefly interested him: ancient German objects, and, as it turned out, Russian women. At home he had a huge number of books about the Germanic peoples, their traditions and their religion. In addition he possessed an ancient Germanic club, two lances, and a helmet with ram's horns. When he read in the newspaper that an ancient Germanic village had been excavated in Brandenburg and could now be viewed by the public, he packed up his treasures right away and drove over. There, outside the gates, he changed his clothes, and made his appearance carrying a lance and sporting a ram's-horn helmet on his head, like a true Germanic tribesman finally returning to his roots in Brandenburg. Even so, he had to pay 30 marks to get in.

I had met him in the Frankfurter Tor underground station. Markus was trying single-handedly and with true heroism to dismantle the precision electronic scales, one of those weight machines that gives you a printed card. He wanted to take it home. I had always wondered how those machines were built, so we ended up taking it apart together. Afterwards I went to see him once or twice in his apartment on Senefeldstrasse. On one occasion Markus asked me how ancient history was dealt with in Russia. 'None too well,' I told him honestly. 'It's as if our cultural roots had been cut. The ties between the generations are really buggered. What passes for folklore is mainly in the hands of single women who band up in troupes and tour the world singing and dancing.'

One such brigade of women happened to be visiting Berlin at the time. They were dancing and singing on the stage of the Russian House in Friedrichstrasse. The company was called The Birch, because the songs praised birch trees and other distinctive Russian trees. 'As for the true history of Russia, needless to say it has been kept from us,' I told Markus.

'It's just the same here, the same here,' he replied. He decided that he simply had to see the Birch collective. We went together. It was a big stage, and twenty young women, wearing traditional headgear, were performing a round dance.

Markus was entranced. I realised that ideally he would have liked to invite the entire company home with him. And, since we were practically the only audience, the women on stage had noticed us too.

After the show, Markus wanted to enthuse to the Birch collective in person, with me as interpreter. In less than an hour, five of us were in a taxi on our way to Markus' place. The three Birch girls who came with us were called Katja, Olga and Sweta, and so far their only glimpse of Berlin had been from the hotel window. On the way we bought the national drinks of both countries—three bottles of vodka and a crate of beer. Mixing these two subsequently turned out to be a big mistake. Once the second bottle of vodka was lying empty under the table, Markus decided to enlighten the women on the subject of ancient Germanic history. He got his favourite lance out of the cupboard and waved it about under our noses. One of the girls, Katja or Sweta, instantly imagined she was being attacked. At lightning speed she disarmed Markus and threw the lance out of the window. Markus was beside himself with fury. The two of them raced out of the flat, and the rest of us followed. The neighbours called the police, who turned up and tried to broker peace. At the police station, Markus brought a charge of trespassing against the girl. She for her part brought no fewer than seven charges against him, among them attempted rape and murder. Markus yelled that it was all the Birch Woman's fault.

The police officers dealt with the case unbureaucratically and suggested we beat it, fast, in different directions. They kept Markus handcuffed to the door of the station, till he had calmed down. There he was approached by a man who introduced himself as a reporter from the *Berliner Zeitung* and said he happened to be passing and was wondering what had happened. 'Crap,' Markus answered pithily. The reporter did not linger but fished out his camera and took a few photographs of him. Next day, there was Markus in handcuffs in the *Berliner Zeitung*. Underneath the picture was a single sentence: 'The Berlin police are cracking down on Yugoslavian criminals.'

Double Lives in Berlin

Where I come from, life is unfit to be lived. Given the strong winds and poor public transport, whatever you plan to do turns into an immensely arduous undertaking. At the age of fourteen you are already incredibly weary, and you don't get a proper break to recover till you're forty-five. Very often people go out shopping and don't come back, or else they write a novel and on page 2,000 they suddenly realise how confusingly out of hand the whole thing has got and start all over again from the beginning. It is a timeless life, one of the great achievements of which is the chance to die in one's own bed.

Here things are quite different. Here, depending on circumstances, you may lead more than one life simultaneously, your own and somebody else's. For those who like that kind of double life, Berlin is the ideal city. Nothing here is as it seems. Recently I saw the woman at my bank who advises customers on investments—a pleasant, plump person sporting a name badge reading 'Wolf' on her blouse—dancing in an audio ballet at one of Berlin's countless dance theatres. Every other evening she slips into a Perspex tutu with recording and playback units built in. Then Frau Wolf gives a little waggle of her backside, and her movements are registered and translated into a sort of music that comes from the tutu and provides the rhythm to which the entire company dance. Like one possessed, Frau Wolf leaps about the stage with all the other investment advisers, utterly oblivious. Last year the ladies competed at an audio ballet festival in Japan and won a prize.

I met Herr Heisenberg at the job centre back when I was long-term unemployed. His task was to persuade people in callings it was hard to find jobs in, such as actors, directors or theologians, to retrain for another profession. Herr Heisenberg had a tendency to go on and on about what was sensible. 'I am a great fan of art,' he told me, 'and I'm delighted that it's on view at every street corner these days. But my urgent advice to you is to take up a sensible job as a businessman, say, or a joiner.' The colour of his tie perfectly matched the wallpaper in his office. Heisenberg sounded very convincing and put me in a thoroughly bad mood for the rest of the day. It so happened that I had promised to show my mother Berlin's night life that evening. She had been waiting for this for a long time. Shortly after midnight we fetched up in a gay bar in central Berlin, and there I told my mother about my frustrating talk at the job centre. Suddenly I noticed Heisenberg in a corner. He was wearing jeans, a buff leather jacket and a fat gold chain around his neck. A Thai boy was sitting on his lap, laughing. 'By the way, that's him over there, my job counsellor,' I told my mother. She looked round cautiously, then shook her head and said it was 'disgusting'.

Last summer an acquaintance of mine, a Russian businessman named Hensel who is in the wholesale car trade selling German vehicles into Sweden, was surprised by a rhinoceros and almost trampled underfoot. His friend, a senior engineer with Siemens, had provoked the rhino, while

Hensel, suspecting nothing, went on with breakfast preparations a hundred yards away. At first the rhino attacked the Siemens engineer, who, accustomed by his profession to taking rapid action in complex situations, promptly climbed the nearest tree. Thereupon the rhino moved on to the car dealer, sending the jam flying.

Hensel was confined to a hospital bed for several weeks, and his journey of pilgrimage to the Himalayas came to nothing. He now plans to fit in some kind of pilgrimage on his next safari in the spring. The two friends are both of the opinion that nowadays you can only have adventures of this kind in Africa. True, there may not be any crazed rhinos in Berlin, but here in the jungle of the big city dangers lurk everywhere too. The service industry can make the wildest of dreams come true, even by phone. Thus the rumour persists that the glass windows of the Lafayette store, weighing tons, didn't come crashing down into Friedrichstrasse because of shoddy building work* but at somebody's behest. Thanks to the quick thinking of a man in the street, nobody was hurt. The windows were smashed, true, but the evening was unmarred by anything worse.

* This was a big news story in Berlin. The huge, new glass windows of the Lafayette building fell out spontaneously and mysteriously – seemingly because of their exceptional weight.

Lichtenberg Station

My old acquaintance Andrei, proprietor of what is probably the only Russian chain of grocery stores in Berlin, Kasatschok, is planning to give up his business, which is going well, and emigrate to America with his family.

He is keeping the reasons for this decision to himself. Perhaps he has fallen foul of German tax law, or maybe Europe isn't the place for his imperialist ambitions. The fact is that, in recent times, Andrei had evolved into an unscrupulous businessman.

And yet just nine years ago we laid the foundation stone of his career, together and quite innocuously, when we moved from Moscow to Berlin.

Our first place of business was outside the door of the entrance hall at Lichtenberg railway station. At the time, Andrei, Mischa and I were living in a one-room apartment in the aliens' home at Marzahn. Mischa and I did not yet have any definite aims in life and liked to hang around in the kitchen of an evening, playing the guitar. Andrei was a pretty good guitar player too, but he already had a target he was aiming for: come hell or high water, he wanted to be a millionaire. After all, he was quite a bit older than we were. He was already thirty-one.

His first idea of how to get rich fired us with enthusiasm. In those days we were given 180 marks pocket money each month by the German government, and Andrei promised us three times as much. We pooled our money and went in to Wedding at seven in the morning. There we bought three rucksack-loads of canned Hansabier and Coke at the local Aldi store, and schlepped the stuff off to Lichtenberg station. At that time, capitalism had not quite reached those parts; we were pretty much the pioneers. We sold the cans for DM 1.20. Other pioneers were there alongside us: an East German family selling ham and egg rolls. They were very proud of the fact that they prepared what they sold by hand, and they couldn't stand us because in their eyes we were just money-grabbers out to make a fast mark. The family knew a can of Hansabier cost just 43 pfennigs at Aldi and we were asking for nearly three times as much, Andrei even four times as much, while they had toiled to fix their rolls. Oddly enough, it was these honest folk with their lovingly prepared fare who were sent packing by health department inspectors. The family's hands were too dirty for preparing rolls, their licence had expired, and the rolls were not suitably wrapped. All the while, we were pretending to be the usual railway station boozers, so the inspectors didn't even register us. It never even occurred to them that we were street hawkers too.

Business went well: we had a lot of regular customers, such as the everlastingly thirsty Jehovah's Witnesses and the neatly pressed Scientologists, who went to meet every train from eastern Europe in order to catch the disoriented foreigners off their guard and convert them to their faith on the spot. A lot of arrivals who were making landfall on the shores of capitalism for the first time supposed that the Lord's pamphlet peddlers were part of the package. The bewildered foreigners were our best customers too, as were a pack of gypsies and Africans who were also pursuing their own line of business at the station. And last but not least, the Japanese tourists.

But Mischa and I were too impatient: we did not want to sacrifice more than an hour to business, so we often made special offers, or drank what remained of the merchandise ourselves. Then we would head back to Marzahn, relieved. Often all we had instead of money was a stomach ache, and a light hangover instead of a profit.

With Andrei, things were completely different. He never drank a thing himself, and could hang on at the station half the night to get rid of two unsold cans. If business was not going well he even upped his prices from DM 1.80 to DM 2.50. Andrei had his own sales strategy. He was continually experimenting with the selection he offered. One time he'd buy a kilogram of chewing gum at Aldi as well, and another time two dozen Duplo chocolate bars, which he laid out unassumingly on the ground beside the beer and sold at 50 pfennigs each. He saved his money, lived almost exclusively on muesli, and kept meticulous accounts of his takings and expenses. Before long he had made enough to buy his first TV set, which he himself took personally to Poland by train, to sell at market. He returned with a 100-marks' profit. On his next trip he took a stereo too.

A year later, Mischa and I were still playing the guitar in the kitchen, while Andrei was already opening his first shop in Dimitrowstrasse and owned a Volkswagen. He approached the enterprise in a truly scientific spirit and conducted a survey of the neighbourhood to determine what articles were the main items to have in stock. In accordance with the results, he mainly stocked three things: Jägermeister lager, Berliner Pilsner, and *Bild am Sonntag* newspaper. He was aiming higher, however, and in the end the shop was full of every kind of item, from light bulbs to sewing kits. He also added Russian foods to his range. A short while later he married a woman from St Petersburg, who bore him a son whom he named Mark. Andrei told us that his dream was of a big family, he wanted lots of children. Mischa remarked that he would probably call his second son Pfennig; but, the way things are looking now, I suppose Andrei's next boy is more likely to be called Dollar.

Stalingrad

For some time now, a lot of Russians living in Berlin who would otherwise be perfect candidates for long-term unemployment have had a job once again. The magic word is Stalingrad. Now a major feature film.

In this 180-million-mark movie production by Jean-Jacques Annaud, the Russians are played by Russians. True, Annaud pays the lowest rates in all Europe for film extras, but at least it means that for a while all of them are in full-time employment. Their task is to storm Stalingrad, which has been reconstructed at Krampnitz near Potsdam. At least three Russian actors of my acquaintance claim to have been chosen by Annaud for a lead part, that of the historically authentic sniper Vassily. All three had the honour of a personal audition with the master, and all three have already entered the shooting days in their diaries. As far as I can see, every casting agency in Berlin went looking for actors for *Stalingrad.* I got a call from one of them too: 'Please send us a black-and-white photo of yourself, 30 by 40 centimetres,' a female voice demanded. 'But I'm not an actor,' I objected. 'So what are you?' the voice asked in some surprise; evidently the casting agent supposed that every Russian in Berlin was an actor. 'I'm a caretaker,' I said, in a spirit of protest. 'Fine, ok, send us the photo anyway, black-and-white, 24 by 30 centimetres. Oh and by the way, you wouldn't happen to know some really old Russian woman, say around ninety?' I did happen to know one, but the casting agent already had her name.

This film has been attracting a huge amount of attention even before shooting begins, and not only here. From Moscow I recently had word that Russian movie impresario Nikita Mikhalkov is toying with the idea of making the biggest and most expensive Russian war film of all time, in response to Annaud's project: *The Conquest of Berlin*. At present, I gather, contacts in government and army circles are being made, so that access to funding and permissions poses no problems. The plan is to reconstruct ruined Berlin in the Chechen capital, Grozny, and war veterans will be allowed to play a part. The Russian film, needless to say, cannot be quite so expensive; but the Russians have real cannon and a real civilian population that they can mow down—in other words, they have genuine realism on their side. Mikhalkov has a location in Russia such as Annaud can only dream of.

Doubtless both films will be hugely successful box office hits. After all, there are lots of people who love this sort of thing; America, for instance. Only yesterday a friend of mine who used to be an actress and now handles the Russian telephone sex line in Berlin confirmed as much. Time and again she has Germans calling the number. Recently she had an old man on the line. 'Russian telephone sex?' he asked. 'Fine. But none of this "I'm going to undress slowly just for you" or "My that's a big one"—none of that crap! I don't like that. Listen: it's 1943, a minefield near Stalingrad. It's freezing cold and the air smells of gunpowder. In the distance you can hear the artillery thundering away. Your name is Klawa, you're blonde, fat, and lying in the snow. All you're wearing is army boots and a cap. I'm in the uniform of an SS stormtrooper captain and I'm coming to get you. And—action!'

How I Was an Actor Once

We'd best give German cinema a bit of a helping hand, we reflected. United we are strong: director Annaud, that Mummy woman, Shakespeare in Love, the private detective in Roger Rabbit, a Bulgarian magician, two hundred extras and me, all of us employed in the making of *Stalingrad*.

At five in the morning we all assemble at Fehrbelliner Platz. From there we are driven by bus to Krampnitz, to the Kruschev headquarters. I know Kruschev, he was the comedian in the Roger Rabbit film. He is sitting on a stool in the recreation room, on his own and bored. I go up to him: 'How are you? How's Roger Rabbit?' Instantly the director's assistant chases me out of the room. Extras aren't supposed to talk to the stars, she says. What nonsense! Not much is going on today. About forty extras, mainly Russians, are wandering around the site. The screwing scene has to be shot today, they tell me. The third within a week already. Everyone has got the message by now: this war movie isn't so much about the battle, and all the tanks and aircraft are really no more than a backdrop to a complicated love story. Tanya, the Mummy woman, is in love with the sniper Vassily, but is sleeping with

Shakespeare in Love, and does so whenever there are loud explosions outside. Meanwhile, Roger Rabbit is suffering the pangs of loneliness. He loves Tanya too and is forever ranting against Stalin, as if it were his fault that Roger is always on his own.

I almost missed breakfast. It is ready on the tables from as early as six o'clock. Today there are bacon and eggs, rolls with cold cuts, coffee and tea. All the extras are delighted, and prepare for long waits spent sitting around. For many Russians, *Stalingrad* has provided something for the entire family to do. The men are in the battle scenes, the women play secretaries on Kruschev's staff, and the children hang around.

Before the love scene starts, HQ is bombarded good and proper. That is how things are done in Stalingrad. While the bombardment is in progress, I have to hide behind a big kitchen cupboard in terror. The cupboard is a valuable piece of furniture, a genuine antique, full of packets of bay leaves with Russian printed on them. The bay leaves make little sense in the context, but the props mistress cannot read the writing anyway; all that matters is that it's Russian. The bombardment calls for elaborate technical expertise. One technician shakes the kitchen cupboard while another sprinkles dust on me. The assistant director is dissatisfied. 'You're not scared enough,' she tells me. 'Just imagine that this could be the last day of your life. Can't you make the kind of face you would make in that situation? Not so stiff!' 'For 13 marks an hour I'm not going to start pulling faces,' I protest. 'It's quite enough if I sit behind this bay-leaf cupboard covered in dust. If you want faces pulled, you have Roger Rabbit.' A row over wages erupts. In the end someone else is brought in to take my place, and I head off to join the other extras, who are playing cards outside.

The screwing scene is filmed as shadow-play on the side of a tent. Outside the tent, we soldiers are playing cards. The Bulgarian magician shows us some card tricks and tells us how the German federal government paid 35,000 marks to get him out of a Bulgarian prison in the old days. 'A bargain,' he declares. A German extra retorts that it was a waste of good money. The Russians maintain a diplomatic silence. The assistant director comes over to ask if anyone is willing to bare his backside to the camera for an extra 250 marks. The Russians are embarrassed, and so is the Bulgarian. Only the German declares himself willing. His behind is filmed by two cameras, one from the rear and one from the side. The content of the scene is this: while the Mummy woman is in the tent enjoying the transports of passion with Shakespeare in Love, the card players outside are having their own kind of fun. The loser has to blow out five candles with a fart. That's how it is with these savage Russian customs. The thirty soldiers are supposed to find it wildly funny, but in reality everyone is simply ashamed.

In the Trenches at Stalingrad

'I'd much rather have played a German officer,' Grisha says to me, cramming black caviare into his mouth. Grisha is the one Russian actor who has managed to land a reasonable part in the *Stalingrad* film, *Enemy at the Gates*. He plays a Soviet political official, he has three days of shooting, and he makes 10,000 marks for it.

Grisha is a wise man: 'The Germans need protecting in this laughable film production,' he says. We are sitting in the Kruschev staff quarter; shooting has just finished. Yesterday they shot 'Russian officers at breakfast' here. The props mistress had bought any amount of fish at the KDW, plus several kilograms of caviare at 4,000 marks a kilo and fifty bottles of vintage Soviet champagne. The breakfast table was fully laden with these and other choice delicacies. But the actors ate and drank none of it. When they were done, the props people prepared the next scene: 'After the Russians have eaten.' The caviare and fish were distributed evenly around the whole table and then mushed as if wild boars had trampled them underfoot. To conclude, they poured the champagne over the spread, so that even the stupidest movie-goer would realise that the barbarians had been having an orgy in the midst of the war.

So now Grisha and I are standing by the table, discreetly helping ourselves before the whole lot ends up in the bin. 'The Germans need protecting,' Grisha goes on, 'because when all's said and done they suffered an honourable defeat back then. Now it's the end of February and outside it is already 14 degrees above zero. In Stalingrad, at twenty-four below, they can't have had an easy time of it in their thin uniforms. It was tantamount to a suicide mission. They ought to have stormed the KDW instead.' Suddenly my friend coughs. He has swallowed another of Kruschev's liver spots. Bob Hoskins, who is playing the part of Kruschev, is always losing his fake liver spots. He has a very mobile face, and has to be freshly made up by a whole team of make-up women every hour. They consult a fat American book about Kruschev which details the Russian's liver spots exactly.

'A pity they're tipping the champagne away,' observes Grisha. 'But what the hell, the Americans don't drink champagne, they prefer beer.' 'The Russians like beer as well,' I reply. 'The Russians drink everything, and they don't wait to be asked twice,' says Grisha. In the mean time I had been carrying on putting away Kruschev's breakfast, and had reached my limit. 'No more of this false modesty, we can't let all these good things be thrown away. We owe it to our fathers who stormed Stalingrad,' Grisha the agitprop officer says provocatively. 'The whole of this film production is designed to be wasteful. They'll buy fresh stuff and then throw it all away again. Why do you suppose they are making this film at all?' I ask my friend, bent on enlightening him. 'Why do you think? Stupidity, of course,' he declares. 'No, schadenfreude,' I claim: 'a characteristic feature of Western civilisation.' I'll have to tell my American colleagues.' Grisha reflects for a moment and goes on chewing: 'What's the English for schadenfreude?' 'I don't know. We'll have to look in the dictionary.' A little later we find a German-English dictionary in the props department. The English for schadenfreude, it turns out, is schadenfreude.

Political Correctness

Modern society is destroying the traditional ways in which people deal with each other. To prevent social life from becoming altogether intolerable, democratic states invent new artificial rules. The latest thing in this field is known as political correctness.

For instance, in the US, that country of unlimited laws, women have for some time been able, if they should so wish, to ride the New York subway with their breasts bared, a spin-off of equal rights for women. At the same time, other passengers are forbidden to stare at their nude tits. This would be politically most incorrect: it would be a violation of the private sphere, and could result in charges being brought.

Two Russian actors are in the production of *Titus Andronicus* at the Berliner Volksbühne. In this bloodiest and most violent of Shakespeare's plays, the cast are forever being mutilated. Great numbers of legs, hands, tongues and other vital body parts are cut off on stage. The principal villains, the barbarians, are played by Russians. Because of course everyone knows that barbarians come from a long way off and speak with a Russian accent.

In New York, people with Down's Syndrome are not to be referred to as such. The politically correct term is 'alternatively gifted persons'. There are a lot of American books and Hollywood movies that deal with this topic of alternative giftedness. An entire cultural industry has arisen from it. As a rule, many alternatively gifted people work in department stores or supermarkets, where they stand at the checkout packing the goods into bags. They are invariably pleasant and instantly put you in mind of Forrest Gump or Rain Man. But the New York rain men have one curious habit: when they pack your bag, they stow the soft fruits and vegetables at the bottom, and the two-litre cans and whisky bottles at the top. The Americans, who have got used to quite a bit in the name of political correctness by now, don't let it vex them in the slightest. Quite the contrary: because they are modern, enlightened people, they have complete understanding of what might initially seem the topsy-turvy logic of the alternatively gifted. The Down's people aren't doing it to ruin the pleasure other people take in their consumer practices; it's just that they want to touch the things that look and feel good first, such as the warm red tomatoes and red peppers, and the last things they touch are the cold, dead, inert olive oil cans and bottles. They do not assess things by their weight but according to other, arguably aesthetic criteria.

In one Berlin theatre, a black African actress recently asked the director what had been in his mind when he offered her the part of the Devil. The director observed that he had been thinking of certain characteristics of Woman. 'It's very odd,' said the actress; 'I've been living in Germany for five years, I've been in three theatre productions, and every time I've had to play the Devil.' 'Take it easy, Marie-Hélène,' said the director, stroking her sizeable behind and smiling indulgently, 'it's got absolutely nothing to do with the fact that you happen to be black.'

The Russian Disco

A Full Eyewitness Account by the Organiser:

On 6 November in the Zapata bar a dance event with Russian hits was held for the first time. The motto was 'Wild Dancing to Mark the Anniversary of the Great October Revolution'. Thanks to the plugs on Radio MultiKulti, the Russian Disco was met with widespread enthusiasm, and large numbers showed up.

The Zapata was jam packed. The wife of the organiser, who was on the door, calculated that in all three hundred people paid to get in. The price was 7 marks and the organiser's wife rigorously demanded it of all comers. Unfortunately, rather too many Russians proved uncooperative in this respect, and wanted to dance wildly for nothing, but not all of them were equally resourceful in their arguments. So in the end people paid anything from four to seven marks, depending on their appearance and degree of stubbornness. It was a young and international crowd. Also present was a Spanish TV team that had probably lost its way in Oranienburger Strasse and happened upon the disco unexpectedly. A group of erstwhile Japanese tourists who had been missing in the area for more than six months suddenly reappeared too. The local editor of the *Berliner Zeitung* found it all very exciting and insisted that only the Russians could throw a party like this. Even so, she soon felt a little queasy and kept on asking for herbal drinks such as camomile tea or peppermint tea, which are not available at the Zapata.

On the whole, despite the large number of paying guests, the manager of the Zapata was disappointed in the Russians, because they did not drink as heavily as he'd been hoping. The turnover at the bar could have been better, and the five crates of some curious drink called 'Pushkin Light' which he had had in store for more than a year and was planning to get rid of at last did not sell well. But since the majority of those present got drunk pretty quickly nonetheless, the manager suspected that many of the Russians had brought their drinks with them, according to the ancient tradition; nor was he so very wrong.

At intervals the organisers tried to convey to the dancing multitudes the meaning and significance of the October Revolution, and to communicate the values of internationalism and of harmony among the peoples of the world—for instance, when announcing what is known as the White Dance, when the ladies choose their gentlemen. Numerous solo Russian women encountered their destiny, meeting new friends or partners or interesting people. Thus the female editor-in-chief of the Russian section of MultiKulti clinched four hours of wild dancing by hooking a powerfully built, balding man, about six foot two inches tall, who introduced himself as a manager with Pro Sieben television. When she attempted to carry him off home with her, though, the man vanished into thin air. Thereupon the editor heaped odium on that station, declaring that this was the third Pro Sieben manager she had met in the last year who had suddenly disappeared. Another woman met a young film-maker from Potsdam, and now he calls her every day.

Even after six hours of wild dancing, no one had any intention of leaving, but the team of DJs were utterly exhausted and at half-past four they stopped the music. Since the event was such a success, the organisers are planning another disco evening for the near future: 'Russian Disco – Wild Dancing on Christmas Eve.' And you are all cordially invited.

Yours Most Sincerely,

The Organiser

The Women's Spring Festival

The Women's Club, one of the most active institutions in the Jewish community in Potsdam, recently threw a big spring party, since the weather was getting milder. Their choice of a suitable venue fell upon the modern Protestant church at Kirchsteigfeld, where the distinctly tolerant vicar understands pretty much everything and has long since ceased to be surprised by anything at all.

The event began with a fashion show, as advertised. A famous woman designer and active member of the Women's Club had created a spring and summer collection for the occasion, for self-assured young girls. The dresses were all cut on the topless principle. The designer had invested a good deal of imagination in her collection, but not much material. To applause from the audience, the bare-breasted girls strolled down a catwalk built by the Women's Club's menfolk. The programme informed you that this spring and summer collection had already been presented in New York, Sydney and London, in other words pretty much worldwide, and had been given a rapturous reception everywhere. The fashion show was followed by a performance by a children's ballet troupe called

Goose Pimples, whose dance of the little swans threw the audience into even greater transports of delight. The only one left cold by the performance was the vicar. Doubtless the man of Kirchsteigfeld had seen a thing or two in his life.

Next after the children's ballet was the mixed choir of Jewish immigrants and Russian Germans with their new programme, 'We're doing fine'. They sang satirical verses of their own composition, a traditional Russian custom. These satires always possessed great social significance in Russia, because they often expressed the voice of the people, in exaggerated form. In the choir's satires, various officials at the Potsdam welfare office and immigration authority were exposed to criticism, and the Jewish immigrants and Russian-Germans were exhorted to stick together and consolidate their friendship. After all, the two groups shared a common past, the Soviet Union.

The next entertainer on the bill was a man who for some time has been known to the Potsdam immigrant scene by the nickname 'the Translator'. For years this man has been translating the most famous of all Russian poets, Pushkin: to be exact, the selfsame poem over and over again. It is entitled 'To the Poet'. In his day, Pushkin dedicated the poem to himself. Now the Translator declaimed it in a new, modern version in which everything rhymed: 'Do not care for applause, my friend, / Stay cool until the very end. / Be free of spirit as you wend / Your way, and earn your dividend.'

To conclude the Jewish community's Women's Club's event, everyone present dined together: the bare-breasted girls, the children's ballet, the Jewish community's mixed choir, the Pushkin translator, and a number of passers-by who had spotted the lights still on in the Kirchsteigfeld church at that hour of the night. All of them gathered around the table with the food and drink. There was enough lebkuchen and cheap kadarka red wine for a regiment. Only the Protestant vicar sat in a corner on his own. Even when the last belly dance was over and the stragglers finally went home, he did not move. No doubt he remained sitting there half the night, pondering everything that had happened that day.

The Columbo of Prenzlauer Berg

At nine in the morning, someone rang the doorbell. I leapt out of bed, pulled on my red underpants and opened up. It was the police again. An elderly man in a green uniform, with a big pistol in a holster and a slightly skewed gaze. I already knew him, the Columbo of Prenzlauer Berg. 'Do you speak German?' he asked me, as he always did. 'But of course, Inspector. Come on in.' Unconsciously I promptly slipped into the role of a murderer. 'I hope I'm not disturbing you,' murmured Columbo, seeing my half-dressed family in the kitchen. My three-year-old daughter instantly suggested he play chickens with her. 'No, darling, Uncle didn't come to play.'

The problem was that one night a good three months before, a gun had been fired in our yard. The bullet had made a hole in the window of an unoccupied apartment on the third floor. At the time, my wife and I were watching television. 'Missing in Action' was on Pro Sieben. On screen, Chuck Norris, who was seriously annoyed because his family had gone missing in South East Asia, was unleashing death and terror on the Vietnamese. Half the people who live in our building in Schönhauser Allee are Vietnamese, and half are

Latinos who never tire of dancing to 'Guantanamera'. Our building is quite loud itself, and outside it is of course loud anyway. On television, Chuck Norris was just busy liquidating Vietnamese by the dozen, but the Vietnamese weren't so keen on the treatment they were getting and were shooting back. Above us, the Latinos were having a wild time, playing 'Guantanamera' time and again. Outside, train drivers were glad to be driving the last underground trains of the night to the depot. And some time or other a shot was fired in the yard. No one really noticed.

Quite likely Columbo is taking the whole business much too seriously. Ever since, he has been seen in our yard every week. He shambles to and fro, measuring distances and poking around in the fallen leaves. Now and then he stops in some corner and stares meditatively up at the sky. He's forever calling on someone or other in the building. With every day that passes, he knows more about us, and now even the colour of my underpants is no longer a secret to him. 'Perhaps it was an air rifle?' I venture, hesitantly trying to play the affair down. 'It must have been a damned big air rifle!' he retorts, and screws up both eyes, offended. You can tell he is hot on the trail of the villain. 'Has anything unusual struck you recently?' he asks us. Even this simple enquiry is desperately embarrassing. How on earth am I to explain to him that practically all the tenants in our building look like rabid desperadoes? No, I tell Columbo nothing of the sort. Better keep it to myself. I pretend to be deliberating on what 'unusual' might mean: 'No, I can't say I've noticed anything.' The inspector takes his leave: 'Here, this is my card.' In the doorway he pauses once more. 'Oh, by the way, I almost forgot: is that pushchair in the yard yours?' 'No, it's not ours.' I told him as much once before, by mistake, and now I have to stick adamantly to that version. Once he's gone, I ask my wife to bear in mind, just in case he should stop by again, that our pushchair in the yard is not ours. A little later it starts to snow outside. I look out of the window. Columbo is in the yard yet again—and he's delighted. He's delighted! I can see why. Soon it will be winter and there will be snow everywhere, in which criminals will leave tell-tale trails. Now he'll get every one of us, sooner or later.

Berlin Guidebooks

For some time now, Berlin has been considered by Russian travel agencies to be some kind of insider tip for the wealthy. You can have a really wild time there, they say. In one Russian guide to Berlin, the tour operators' slogan runs: 'Raise your very own personal flag on the new German Reichstag—see Berlin and conquer it!'

My old friend Sasha, who studies German at the Humboldt University, was recently asked to update one of these Russian guidebooks to Berlin. Nothing dramatic, just a few up-to-the-minute tips such as Potsdamer Platz and such-like. In despair he came to me. Wealthy Russians do not have much time, and for that reason old guides to the city allocate just one day to it or at the most three. Everything has to be rushed. If the tourist is particularly pedantic and opts for a five-day visit, he is told to go to the devil, i.e. to Potsdam—out of Berlin. 'A delightful location with lots of sculpture, fast food outlets and waterfalls,' the Russian version of Potsdam reads. 'Especially recommended is Sanssouci, the palace built by King Frederick II in 1744. The canteen there is well worth a visit too, for the roast suckling pig with bacon dumplings and red cabbage with apple. The picture gallery in the palace is also worth seeing; the Caravaggios and Raphaels are genuine, but not for sale. One warning: even if you are extremely thirsty, do not drink from the waterfall, as this might cause sickness.'

The tone of the tips for shorter stays is similar, a mixture of art book pathos and culinary handbook. In the case of one-day visits, the speed is drastically accelerated. From the Europa Center, the Russian races to the KDW department store to try the deep sea prawns. The KDW is designated 'superb' and 'particularly good value for money'. Then he moves on to the Brandenburg Gate, which is described as 'a superb remnant of the Berlin Wall'. In the eastern part of the city one is urged to try a little something too. The 'German steaks', which is what the Russians call bockwurst sausages, are declared to be 'superb' in the east, and 'outstanding' in flavour. The wine, however, is 'not as sweet as it was before the fall of the Wall, which really was a long time ago'. Then it's on to the Reichstag, where the Russian can raise his very own personal flag—whatever the author may have meant by that.

Now Sasha's dilemma was that he had to have some bright idea about Potsdamer Platz. All evening we sat there in our kitchen. Strange. We couldn't think of a thing to say about Potsdamer Platz. 'A superb future in the old heart of the city?' I suggested in desperation. The last time I was there, I was approached three times in half an hour by security officers. The first time my shoelace had come undone and I had knelt down to tie it. The next second he was standing beside me: 'What's the problem?' 'Thanks, everything's just fine,' I answered, and went on my way. Looking for a toilet, I went into one of those superb residential and recreational developments that are all over the place there. Instantly another officer was at my side: 'What's cooking?' 'No sweat,' I said, and was out of there. 'Be sure to visit Potsdamer Platz, the realm of the rich. In the bars and casinos here you are sure to be rid of your hard-earned money in next to no time and without the slightest effort.' That, as things turned out, was what we ended up with. By now it was getting late. We went out and dived into the depths of Prenzlauer Berg, in search of a drink.

The New Jobs

The millennium is over. A good reason for a fresh start. The whole of humanity is longing for a change. Many of our acquaintances are already looking for a new flat, new friends, new jobs. Indeed Martin, who sells *Motz*, has embarked on a proper career. Having spent months annoying passengers on route 2 of the underground with his 'Hi, I'm Martin, I'm selling this magazine in aid of the homeless, one mark goes to me, have a pleasant journey', he recently appeared before them in a new guise altogether: 'Hi, I'm Martin, tickets please.'

Our friend Lena, who was completely dissatisfied with her job as an aerobics instructor, retrained as a graphic designer. She'd sent off dozens of job applications before, at last, one company replied and invited Lena to an interview. She prepared thoroughly, buying new American eyelashes made of extra-long mink hair from a specialist cosmetics boutique, with a special extra-powerful gum meant to prevent the lashes from slipping when she blinked or ran. In the interview, Lena batted her lashes vigorously, up and down they flapped, but all in vain. The manager on the other side of the table seemed blind and insensate. The coffee cup in his hand bore the words 'Who gives a toss?' Vaguely he promised Lena to call her some time. After the interview, Lena had a panic attack: she couldn't open her eyes properly any more. The extra-long American mink eyelashes had got knotted and Lena was effectively half blind.

Back home she realised that she had no solvent for the gum. And things were even worse than that: to remove the extra-powerful gum with which the extra-long lashes were glued on, you needed an extra-powerful solvent that you could only buy in the KDW department store. Lena turned up at our place looking like a forest sprite with her eyes gummed shut. She was at her wits' end. I had to go to the KDW for her to procure the means of her salvation. Now she can see clearly again, but the bloke from the computer company still hasn't been in touch.

A while ago I had an interesting job too. 'We're looking for a Russian speaker to say ten words in Russian for us. It pays 100 marks.' The male voice on the telephone sounded perfectly respectable. 'What sort of words?' I speculated on my way to the recording studio in Manteuffelstrasse. 'Not abuse, I hope.' When I arrived, all became clear: a Polish scientist had invented a new fangled gynaecological implement that would completely replace the gynaecologist. And it could speak, in three languages: German, English and Russian. So now this miraculous gadget will be regaling the women of the twenty-first century with my voice in Russian: 'Container is full', 'Container is empty', 'Air bubble!'

'Why do you sound so glum?' the studio engineer asked in an offended tone. 'I thought these were things that were going wrong,' I answered. 'It's sad if the container's empty, say.' 'Rubbish! It's wonderful! 'Container is empty! It's fantastic! You can go home!'

The job was fun. The engineer assured me he would hire me again when the next gadget came along. It is a speaking acupuncture machine, and one thing is that the Russian will have to be spoken with a slight Chinese accent. Though no date has been fixed yet, I was able to take the new text home with me to practise. I read it through on the underground. The very first sentence filled me with enthusiasm: 'We shall succeed in everything!' the machine declares.

The Radio Doctor

Russians living in Berlin do not trust German doctors. They are too self-confident, they always know the answer even before the patient sets foot in the surgery. For every ailment in the world they instantly have the right medicine to hand, for every one of the patient's problems a solution. That can't be right! The kind of doctor Russians will respond to must share the patient's fear of the illness, comfort him, stand by him day and night, listen to all his stories about his wives, children, friends and parents, and if at all possible agree with the diagnosis the patient himself has already arrived at. It is also most important that he should have a good command of Russian, otherwise he will be unable fully to enter into the depths of the patient's suffering. For these reasons, sick Russians invariably look for a Russian doctor. It is easy to find one anywhere.

In Berlin there are Russians in every branch of medicine: dentists and gynaecologists, radiologists and psychologists, dermatologists and cardiologists. The most famous of them all is known as the Radio Doctor. He has nothing to do with radiology. In fact he heals people over the radio, through his programme 'Doctor's Orders', in Russian on SFB 4's Radio MultiKulti, every Monday at half-past six. The Radio Doctor is an old man who moved to Berlin a few years ago from a small town in the Ukraine. In the Sixties he worked in a hospital there. Now he is drawing upon his valuable experience to save human lives on the radio.

His programme always begins the same way: 'Many of our listeners complain of constant headaches. I do not know what the current explanation is, but when I was in the Ukraine there were just two causes: men had headaches because they'd been drinking bad liquor, and women had headaches because they were menstruating.'

The Radio Doctor was immensely successful amongst his Russian listeners. No one else got so many calls or so much fan mail. From these calls and letters, the Radio Doctor selected the topics to be covered in future broadcasts. He knew the answer to every problem. For instance, he told the Russians what to do about spots: 'They'll say Clearasil, but I well recall that petrol is just as good. Diesel is best. Wash your face two or three times a day with diesel and your spots will vanish.'

The Radio Doctor's tried and tested remedy for colds was vodka with pepper and honey. He also knew how to programme the sex of children not yet conceived, and how to eat properly. One of the doctor's favourite subjects is what he calls the Turkish diet. He lives in a Russian ghetto near Hallesches Tor, so the Turkish bazaar is right there on his doorstep all the time.

'Doubtless you have all wondered at some time why Turkish children look so much sturdier than our own, why they are faster on their feet, and why they are such bundles of energy. It is a question of diet, as anyone who goes to the Turkish market will realise. The Turks put away huge amounts of vegetables, small quantities of meat, a lot of easily digested produce: in other words, a diet rich in vitamins. And what about us Russians? Pork roast today, and tomorrow pork roast. We'll never get anywhere like that, comrades!'

The Radio Doctor is held in affection and respect by his fellow broadcasters too. Many confide their most closely held secrets to him and ask his advice. They know the Radio Doctor can help even when everyone else fails. A while ago, a man phoned the station. He wouldn't talk to anyone except the Radio Doctor, and even made the doctor prove to him on the phone that it really was him. 'I have cancer of the bones. The German doctors want to amputate a leg. Do you think it's really essential, or is there maybe some other way?' 'There is always another way,' replied the Radio Doctor. 'Eat lead!' 'Eat what?' 'Eat lead. Lots of lead,' the doctor repeated, and wearily replaced the receiver. Another life saved.

Berlin Portraits

A friend came to see me and asked if I happened to know a beauty surgeon. And how much I thought cosmetic surgery would cost? He wanted a new face. I was pretty shocked, because Sasha had always seemed satisfied with his appearance till that point. Instead, I recommended a child psychiatrist whom I happened to have met recently, and told him the one thing he ought to change about his face was the expression on it—it looked so tragic. Sasha flew into a rage because I wasn't taking his problem seriously, and told me what he had been going through.

His new girlfriend was always taking him to some party or other. One time she had been invited to an exhibition opening at a downtown gallery. On that particular day, Sasha would have preferred to stay at home watching television, and if he had done that none of it would have happened. The premises were packed with an inquisitive art public, and the mood was upbeat. The artist made a personal appearance. Everyone was drinking wine and talking about art. The paintings—or were they photos? Sasha could not remember—clearly emphasised the artist's sexual preference. They showed pricks, hundreds of pricks, wagging affably from the walls. A little merry, Sasha got involved in a conversation with the artist about art, lasting several hours, though he himself was a trained electrician and had no real notion at all. The wine had gone to Sasha's head, and he even offered an analysis of an article in *Focus* magazine, a survey of the arts over the past year, which he had skimmed at the hairdresser's. The artist listened attentively and said things such as, 'What you say is very interesting', or 'You have a fresh way of looking at it', or 'We really should get better acquainted'. Several times his hand wandered between Sasha's legs. By the next day, Sasha had forgotten everything.

A little later, Sasha's girlfriend stopped by, unable to contain her laughter. She had just been having a hot chocolate with another woman at the Café Historia on Kollwitzplatz and they had been looking at the newly painted ceiling. Suddenly she realised that the figure in the middle of the painting was her very own Sasha. He was dressed as Zeus, bare to the waist, and was looking down from on high with a cheeky air. The painting had been done by the prick artist, who earned his living painting murals for bars. Sasha's girlfriend was convinced that the artist had fallen massively for Sasha and was now trying to sublimate his feelings through his creative work.

In the week that followed, Sasha trawled the bars in his neighbourhood and discovered his portrait time and again: there he was in a Mexican restaurant, depicted as a friendly cactus, wearing a sombrero and with a bottle of tequila in his hand; the Egyptian queen on the wall of a trendy pub could have been his twin sister; and in a newly opened sushi bar he made an appearance as a glum fish. The resemblance was astounding. In the end, Sasha became totally paranoid. He began to think everyone in the street was recognising him and pointing to him: look, there goes that fish from the sushi bar. Even the old dragon at the entrance to the Chinese restaurant across the road, which had been there at least ten years, suddenly took on a Sasha-like quality in its facial expression.

Another man in his place might have felt flattered, but my friend was plunged into crisis. I advised him to discuss the problem candidly with the artist. At first Sasha dismissed the suggestion, but then thought better of it. Once they'd got the first round of mutual reproaches behind them, the two men reached an agreement that there were to be no more portraits of Sasha in the Prenzlauer Berg, Berlin Mitte or Friedrichshain districts of town.

The Countess Who Wrote

We received some good news: my old Moscow acquaintance Lena is now the Countess de Carli and lives in a castle near Rome. Lena was always living proof that it takes only hard work and determination and any dream can come true. For years she had been working the Intourist Hotel, in the hope of meeting her prince there. She was already looking for him when Pretty Woman was still in acting school; she waited for him still when the Moscow police were cracking down on prostitution every night; nor did she give up when it had long been clear to everyone else that no prince in his right mind would ever visit Russia of his own free will. Most of the guests at the Intourist Hotel had either committed sex crimes or were planning to. But Lena survived them all.

Now and then she told us perverse tales of her everyday life. Although it was more than ten years ago, many of her stories have stayed in my memory: for instance, the one about the Swede with the boiled egg, or the one about the Japanese with the balalaika, and the Yugoslavian with the silver spoon. But now, Lena is living in Rome, as I have said, and is styled the Countess de Carli. And for a year, she has been a widow too. The old count was not able to enjoy his marriage for long; he had a heart attack in the bath, which put him out of the running for good. His family, one of the most mafioso in Italy, tried at first to blame his death on Lena, and alleged that she had been previously married to someone who also died of a heart attack in the bath. The family were out for revenge, and would long since have had Lena bumped off if it had not been for Julia, the daughter and sole heir. And so Lena lived on unmolested in her castle, with her daughter.

My friend Georg and I had never been to Rome. We'd simply never had the right occasion to make the trip. But visiting Lena in her new role as a widowed countess was all the excuse we needed. We climbed aboard a bus and off we went. Having grown up in the flatlands of Moscow, we instantly felt seasick among the mountains of Italy. Our bus drove up and down, and the two bottles of brandy we had brought along for an emergency were soon empty. Weakened and intoxicated, we alighted in Rome. In the morning mist, Georg promptly fell into what looked like a ditch on a building site but turned out to be the site of an excavation by the Colosseum. A little way off, some Albanian youths were playing football. Georg was determined to join in the game, but the Albanians didn't think much of the idea. Presently some Africans came by selling T-shirts. They claimed to have dug the ditch with their own hands during the night, to help sell their T-shirts with Michelangelos printed on them. Suddenly we found ourselves embroiled in an international incident. Georg swiftly convened a peace conference. In the end the Albanians went home peacefully, and we helped the Africans find a few ancient stones to make the ditch look good. By way of a thank-you they gave us two Michelangelo T-shirts as souvenirs.

We set off to look for Lena's castle. It was already dark when we finally found it. Lena was thrilled to see us. Weary after the long journey, I began with a soak in the bathtub where the count had died. Afterwards I put on his freshly ironed clothes—there were three wardrobes full of them. Lena complained that life as a countess was tedious. She couldn't pick up strangers any more. Her husband's family had hired a bodyguard for her, especially to keep her away from men. In frustration she had turned to literature, and for a year now had been working on an erotic novel into which she was pouring her own experience. I had the honour to be the first reader of her still unfinished work. Lying in the big round marble bath I read her manuscript while Georg, half naked, was picking mandarins from the trees in the nocturnal garden.

The novel was about an English aristocrat who fell in love with a poor village girl and took her with him to his island in the Atlantic. There the Englishman went out riding on a white horse all day long, and was constantly bringing the girl fresh roses. After a while, the two became intimate. Just as it was getting interesting, though, the bodyguard burst in and threw Georg and me out of the house.

The Girl with the Mouse in her Head

Many of the Russians who have settled in Prenzlauer Berg in recent years I already knew back in Moscow. Most of them were artists, musicians or poets: people who have one idea and never develop any further; forever between the hammer and the sickle, already rather shabby, but still in good spirits. In the evenings we would often meet at this or that fellow's place, and spend the whole night in the kitchen, drinking and telling stories, as in the good old days. All of them had seen a lot of life and were bent on telling someone or other about their adventures. The only one who never told us a thing was Ilona, a girl from Samarkand. She had applied for asylum in the Saarland and was forever travelling to and fro between Saarbrücken and Berlin, where she ran the household of a wealthy Russian.

Ilona still had a curious habit: she never took off her cap. She wore her hair extremely short, and also wore unattractive glasses. Very much the dry bread type of woman. She always came to our gatherings and sat in a corner in silence. At times she would get up in the midst of the talk and go into the next room, which was in darkness. But her idiosyncratic behaviour went unremarked, since all of those at the table thought they themselves and the others were a little eccentric anyway. Even so, every newcomer would start by asking Ilona why she never took off her cap. She always had some plausible answer to give, one that invited no further questions. But a time came when we realised that she always gave a different answer. To one enquirer she said that she had been in a car crash and had had stitches on her head. To another she said that her hairdresser had given her the world's worst hair-do. Only Petrov the painter declined to shake her hand as long as she was still wearing her cap. There was something wrong with that girl, he declared. That evening, we all laughed at his intolerant attitude.

My friends Sergei and Irina, an artist couple, were successful in selling some pictures, and I got a contract with a theatre: for the first time, we had some money to spare. We meant to spend it well, and go away somewhere for a few days. To Amsterdam, if possible, or at least Düsseldorf, where a friend of ours had been in a loony bin for years. Sergei and Irina had two children; Sasha was six at the time, and Nicole three. It occurred to us to hire Ilona as a baby-sitter for three days, and we called the rich Russian she worked for. He had no objection, and neither had she, so we gave her some money and off we went. At first the trip went as smoothly as it could, and our friend in Düsseldorf was a lot better now as well. He was not being persecuted by Hitler's children any more, and we took him along with us to Amsterdam. On the way, Sergei phoned home several times. There was no reply. My suggestion that Ilona might be out and about with the children did not reassure the parents.

We drove back as fast as we could. At home the flat was

spick and span and the children were lively and cheerful, but Ilona was nowhere to be found. Sergei established that Ilona had shared the bed with the children although there were two big sofas in the other rooms. 'Why did she do that?' we asked Sasha. 'We had visitors!' he explained with pride. No sooner had we been gone, the children told us, than ten men turned up in two buses, all of them friends of Ilona. She had decided to surprise her friends, and had hidden behind the curtains, but Sasha had helped the men find her. The visitors carried some heavy crates into the flat. In them they had special tools. With these they took Ilona apart, and removed a dead white mouse from her head. Then they put Ilona back together again, ate in the kitchen, and drove off again. All of this Sasha told us while his parents stared in disbelief. I looked out of the window. In the yard, a cat was playing with a dead mouse. The story was gradually beginning to make sense.

Sergei called the wealthy Russian and asked if Ilona had ever removed her cap in his presence. 'No, never.' 'Not even when she slept?' 'Not even when she slept.' Didn't he think that rather strange? 'Not particularly.' 'I am not at all cross with Ilona,' Sergei said into the phone. 'If she shows up, please tell her from me I'd appreciate it if she came by and let me look at her head. Otherwise I'll find her and take a look at her mice myself. I don't have any special tools, but an axe should do the trick just as well,' he said and hung up.

We waited all day, but Ilona never showed up. In the end she appeared at her employer's. She did not want to talk to us, however, and suddenly became aggressive. When Sergei threatened to pull the cap off her head, she finally told us the truth. When her application for asylum had been turned down in the Saarland, a medical institute had proposed a deal. She would make her body available for experiments, with no risk involved, and in return the institute would see that Ilona got a residence permit. At first she agreed to this. Some sort of gauges and gadgets were implanted in her head, and she was given medicine to take. But after a while she became frightened, and ran away from the clinic. According to Ilona, the men in the flat were doctors from the Saarland who wanted their precious technology back. She still wouldn't take her damned cap off, in spite of everything, but now none of us was insisting that she should.

Boring Russians in Berlin

A fellow journalist of mine by the name of Helena has a dangerous job. Every week she writes a column on 'Interesting People in Berlin' for a Russian newspaper published in the city. All day long, Helena is out and about around town, fishing up the 'interesting Russians' from Berlin's murky waters. What is 'interesting' about these Russians is the fact that no sooner has the first interview been conducted than they fall hopelessly in love with Helena and won't give her a moment's peace any more. The young journalist is only interested in these 'interesting' people on a professional basis, however; in her private life she is more attracted to quiet, conventional types whose feet are firmly grounded in reality. 'All these "interesting" characters have got a screw loose,' she frequently complains, 'but I expect that's what makes them interesting.'

Not long ago Helena had a screwy case yet again, one Herr Brukow. He teaches a course of his own invention at the Friedrichshain adult education centre, entitled 'The Castaneda Method'. According to the teacher, the method consists of three elements. The first derives from Herr Brukow's personal experience of the martial arts, experience gained in Magadan in a special unit of the Soviet Ministry of the Interior. The second part has something of Zen and yoga to it. The third involves describing the life and times of Carlos Castaneda. After Helena conducted her interview with Herr Brukow, the teacher went into overdrive. For days on end he kept a watch on her apartment in Prenzlauer Berg, supposedly to protect Helena from evil spirits—by which, no doubt, he presumably meant other interesting Russians. What was more, he was absolutely set on giving her a massage, and declared that in his opinion she moved all wrong. The best was yet to come. Brukow insisted on reading Helena his latest novel, which was the size of a brick and had a lengthy title: *Esoteric Scientific Novel of Life out of the Body.* 'You are undoubtedly a very, very interesting person, Herr Brukow,' Helena told him, 'and I'd be glad to talk more about life out of the body, but if you paw my belly one more time I shall never write a single syllable about you again.'

Another 'interesting Russian', a genuine painter from Karaganda, has been following Helena wherever she goes this past year or so. She wrote an article about him too, entitled 'The Loneliness of the Artist'. In the mean time he has painted flowers on her letterbox and written ambiguous comments on the house wall opposite, in gigantic letters.

And then there is Goldmann, the celebrated dog breeder from Alma-Ata, who was planning to surprise Helena one night with a new breed he had just created, and scared the living daylights out of her in the hallway of her block. Much as Minin the stamp collector had previously done, a man who is quite a celebrity in the world of philately and was bent on making her a gift of his favourite valuable stamp, featuring a death's-head. 'Whyever are interesting people such a lot of bother?' Helena wonders. Ever since the revolting dog of unknown breed fell upon her in the dark hallway she has not been sleeping that well any more. The Castaneda of Höhenschönhausen is beginning to worry her too. She has already received six faxes from him, announcing that he now means to lead the life of the warrior once and for all. Helena is starting to feel veritably surrounded by 'interesting Russians'. She is even thinking of giving up her column, or renaming it 'Boring Russians in Berlin'. I have been trying to talk her out of this. It would be a disaster for the 'interesting people'. After all, they have more need of media support than anyone else.

Learning German

What does modern science have to offer? 'Find the capacity of the resonant circui.' To which all I can say is, find it yourself, and do what you like with it! Recently in a doctor's waiting room I came across a three-page article on quantum mechanics in *Brigitte* magazine. The writer claimed that according to quantum mechanics there was no such thing as time. This is not glad tidings, especially when you've been sitting for over two hours in the doctor's waiting room and getting sicker and sicker. I want nothing to do with the cold world of physics. I'd rather carry on learning German at home—in bed.

Every day for years I have been reading my Russian textbook, *German as the Germans Speak it*, a 1991 teach-yourself book. A comfort to the mind and body. The foreword might alarm some, though, since it describes how terribly complicated the language is: 'In German, a young girl is genderless whereas a potato is not. The bosom is masculine, and all nouns begin with a capital letter.' Thus the Russian lament. But so what? It doesn't trouble me. I have been reading *German as the Germans Speak it* for about eight years and shall doubtless spend another thirty over it. In *German as the*

Germans Speak it, you enter another world, innocent and consoling. The people in the textbook are in clover. They lead harmonious, happy lives that would be impossible in any other textbook: 'Comrade Petrov is a collective farmer. He is a member of the Komsomol. He has three brothers and a sister. All of them are members of the Komsomol. Comrade Petrov is learning German. He works hard at it. Comrade Petrov's flat is on the ground floor. It is a large, light flat. Comrade Petrov is learning German. It is difficult but interesting work. Every morning he gets up at seven o'clock on the dot. He always eats his lunch in the canteen. The weather is always good. On Sundays he goes to the cinema with his comrades. The film is always good. Are you coming? I shall definitely come. You are ill. Let us have tea instead. It is pleasant to take a walk in the woods. We are all for peace. We are against war. Use these books to teach your children!'

If I read this textbook for too long at a stretch, I sometimes begin to feel Comrade Petrov lacks credibility. At such times I put the book aside and, by way of a change, read *German for Foreigners 2*, a German textbook published in Leipzig in 1990 by the Herder Institute: 'Fichtelberg is the highest mountain in the GDR. It is 1,214 metres high. Despite emigration, poverty and danger, Karl Marx was a happy man, because...' Gradually I slide into sleep. I dream of Karl Marx, Comrade Petrov and me up on Fichtelberg at an early hour. The weather is good, the visibility clear. The sun rises and promptly sets again, and flamingos fly slowly south. We talk in German. 'I have a very pleasant flat,' announces Karl Marx. 'It is a large, light flat. I am happy.'

'Me too,' says Comrade Petrov.

'Me too,' I whisper under my breath.

The Language Test

A big wave of naturalisation is about to break. Soon, if the newspapers are to be believed, large numbers of foreigners will have become members of the club known as Germany. Many of my own compatriots, too, are toying with the idea of exchanging their passport to become regular German citizens. The rules governing admission to the club are familiar: you fill in a few forms, supply a few certificates—but beware! As with any big club, hidden traps and ambiguities await you. Many Russians who have been living here for some time clearly still remember what joining the Party used to be like. That too seemed perfectly straightforward on the surface: anyone who was a candidate member for two years and worked hard could become a member. But only the few ever made it. My father, for instance, tried three times to join the Party back in the Soviet Union, in vain. Now he is proposing to take German citizenship. He has been living here for eight years, and this time he does not mean to foul his chances through ignorance. The wily Russians have figured out what it is that plays the deciding role in the naturalisation process: the new, mysterious language test for foreigners, which is currently being introduced in Berlin. With the aid of this test, the powers that be will determine who shall be a German, and who shall not. The document is being kept secret; however, a few excerpts featured in the pages of Berlin's biggest Russian-language newspaper.

My father promptly copied out these excerpts by hand, in order to study them closely. Any child can see that the language test is not so much about a grasp of the language as about the attitudes to life of prospective German citizens. The test presents various situations and asks questions relating to them. There is a choice of three answers to every question. The results are used to draw up a psychological profile of the candidate.

Example I: Your neighbour is always playing loud music late at night. It prevents you from sleeping. You discuss the problem with your partner and wonder what can be done.

Why does the music bother you?

Are you having other problems with this neighbour?

What solutions to the problem do you envisage?

There are three possible answers, a, b and c. Answer c reads, 'You kill the neighbour.' My father can only laugh at this one. He isn't fooled that easily.

Example II: The winter sales (summer sales) have just started. You and your partner are planning to go shopping.

Where and when do you meet?

What do you want to buy?

Why do you want to buy it?

My father isn't stupid. By now he knows perfectly well what a German wants to buy and why.

But the third example is causing him quite a headache. He hasn't yet made out what the subtext is.

Example III: 'Don't go swimming on a full stomach, it's too

dangerous,' parents often tell their children. It is unwise to demand great exertion of the body after a full meal. But on the other hand, no one need be afraid that his physical strength will desert him and he will drown.

Do you like swimming?

Does it ever affect your health?

What do you eat for breakfast?

My father handed me this text and asked what, in my opinion, the Germans might have meant by it. Oh-oh, I thought, this is a really complicated business. All evening I tried to interpret the third example. I even consulted my friend Helmut, considered by my family to be an expert in matters German. But even he could not figure the text out. I am beginning to have a premonition that my father will fail the language test.

Why I Still Haven't Applied for German Citizenship

Here where we live, at the corner of Schönhauser Allee and Bornholmer Strasse, new and ever bigger ditches are dug every night. They are dug by Vietnamese, who have chosen this corner as a good location for selling cigarettes. That, at least, is what I have presumed, ever since I've been seeing them there repeatedly in the light of early morning, spades in hand: two men and a very pleasant woman who has been managing business on the corner for years. 'Why Vietnamese, of all people? Are they creating new storage space for their merchandise?' I wondered on my way to the municipal offices and Herr Kugler.

I had another appointment to apply for German citizenship. My third attempt. Vexing. The first time, everything went very smoothly, I had all the requisite photocopies with me, my financial circumstances looked healthy, all my places of residence since birth, with duration, were listed, I'd accepted that I had to fork out 500 marks in fees, and I'd listed all my children, wives and parents. For two full hours I talked to Herr

Kugler about the meaning of life in the Federal Republic of Germany. But then I fell at a simple fence: preparing a handwritten curriculum vitae. It was supposed to be unconventional, brief, and candid. I took a stack of paper and a ballpoint and went out into the corridor. After about an hour, I had filled five whole pages and still hadn't got as far as kindergarten. 'A handwritten curriculum vitae isn't so easy after all,' I reflected, and started again. By the time I was done I had three drafts, all of them interesting reading but even the best of them getting no further than my first marriage. Dissatisfied with myself, I went home. There I tried to grasp the difference between a novel and a handwritten, unconventional curriculum vitae.

At the next attempt, I failed once again, this time on account of another problem. There was a medium-sized box in which I was supposed to enter my reasons for immigrating into Germany. I racked my brains, but I couldn't think of a single reason. When I migrated to Germany in 1990, I did so absolutely without reason. That evening I asked my wife, who knows the reasons for everything: 'Why on earth did we move to Germany back then?' She claimed we moved to Germany for the fun of it, to see what it was like. But putting it like that wasn't going to help with the matter in hand. The official would think we were applying for German citizenship just for the fun of it too, and not because ... 'Why are we applying for German citizenship?' I asked my wife, but she had already headed out to her driving lesson, to put the fear of death into old ladies out and about in the streets, and drive one instructor after another crazy. My wife has a highly unconventional approach to driving. But that is another story.

Warily, I entered 'Curiosity' as the reason why we had come to Germany, which struck me as sounding more sensible than 'Fun'. Then I copied out my curriculum vitae by hand, from the computer screen. I gathered up everything into a folder and next day went to see Herr Kugler once again. It was early in the day, and still dark, but I wanted to be the first in line, come what may, because these officials cannot handle more than one foreigner a day. And that was when I saw the Vietnamese. They were digging yet again! I went over to have a look. Two men with frustrated expressions were standing in a big hole, and the woman was standing beside them, ranting at them in Vietnamese. The men offered a listless defence. I looked down into the ditch. There was nothing but water in it. Suddenly I realised what it was all about: the Vietnamese had forgotten where they had buried their cigarettes, so now they were looking for them everywhere—in vain.

Suddenly the wind rose, my papers fell out of the folder and into the ditch: that carefully handwritten curriculum vitae, all the reasons for immigrating into Germany, the big questionnaire detailing my financial circumstances—the whole lot splashed into the sopping ditch. I suppose I never shall get German citizenship. But then, why should I?